ELECTRIC GUITARS

an illustrated history

ELECTRIC GUITARS

an illustrated history

CHARTWELL
BOOKS, INC.

A QUANTUM BOOK

This edition published in 2010 by
CHARTWELL BOOKS, INC.
a division of BOOK SALES, INC.
276 Fifth Avenue Suite 206
New York, New York 10001
USA

Copyright © 2010
Quantum Publishing Ltd

QUMEGAS

ISBN-10: 0-7858-2597-5
ISBN-13: 978-0-7858-2597-5

This book is produced by
Quantum Publishing Ltd
6 Blundell Street
London N7 9BH

Publisher: Anastasia Cavouras
Project Editor: Valeria Kogan
Production: Rohana Yusof
Design: Loungefrog

Printed in Singapore
Printed and bound by: Toppan Leefung Printers Ltd

DiMarzio

No. 051 Limited Edition

design by peter solomon

The acoustic guitar as an instrument dates back more than 4000 years ago, originating in what is now Europe and parts of Central Asia. During those times it was constructed principally from animal sinew worked into string which was held tightly over a wooden frame. There is even evidence to suggest the guitar is older still, back so far as ancient Egypt and Babylon. The guitar has an enduring simplicity that belies the lifelong journey that is mastering its playing. There have been many to attempt the task of taming it, though very few have succeeded. Those that do are music legends.

The guitar has traveled the world over; taking on the characteristics of every culture and people it touches, gaining in craftsmanship and tone, taking on new shapes as it does so. In our modern era of the 21st century there has never been more diversity in the building, playing, and distribution of the guitar and it has truly taken on a world shape where it is recognized as a primary instrument in the genres of flamenco, rock 'n roll, and jazz among many others.

As musical styles shifted and morphed a need arose that previous body designs and time-honored craftsmanship techniques were not able to satisfy. It was the dawn of the big band era and guitars players of that time were having trouble getting the volume of their acoustic guitars over instruments such as trumpets and saxophones that the larger traveling bands employed. Many innovations were attempted, from steel body guitars to larger body designs. It was these big band/jazz guitarists that first began to electrify their guitars.

The first hollow-bodied acoustic instruments turned electric with tungsten steel pickups were made by the Rickenbacker Company in 1931. One of the first solid body electric guitars was built by Les Paul and heralded the coming of a new musical age. The electric guitar would quickly become the tool of many frustrated teens and budding musicians, who were able to pick one up cheaply as opposed to the acoustic guitar which was often more expensive and took longer to make.

It was the electric guitar that brought the blues to rock 'n roll in the 1950s and '60s which caused an explosion in musical creativity and diversion of styles. It was also the birth of the guitar hero: Jimmy Page, Eric Clapton, Jimi Hendrix. There were other firsts happening around this time as well. The electric guitar grew up right along with the rise of television, and was brought into just as vibrant a visual palate as its sounds created. The modern age proved to be the perfect storm for the electric guitar which proved to be the instrument of choice for the American youth. It had a certain testosterone about it, a singular accessibility that other instruments lacked. The electric guitar created a limitless realm of possibility that has yet to be fully mined, for each time technology advances, the ceiling on the possibilities for the instrument gives way to new possibilities. What remains to be seen is how great an impact the digital era of the 21st century will have on an instrument that has woven its way very quickly into our social consciousness.

High Tech: XOX the Handle. Designed by renowned luthier Peter Solomon, this guitar is made of carbon fiber and won the 2006 Design Award.

Andersen Stringed Instruments is the brainchild of Steve Andersen, who began the art of guitar making in the early 1980s. He is an independent luthier, building instruments directly to the consumer outside the realms of a large corporate distribution machine. Andersen is a testament to the myriad skills that go into the running of a business that sells musical instruments as well as the skills that go into the crafting them. "I never would have imagined the breadth of skills I've had to learn (and am still learning) along the way," writes Andersen on his website andersenguitars.com. "Photography, bookkeeping, tool design and construction, metalworking, advertising, customer relations, computer skills, tonewood harvesting and processing, carbon graphite composites and electronics are all skills I've acquired over the years. Of course, learning such things has improved my instruments, but if I'd had a clue when I first ventured into guitar making, I might have opted for something a bit 'easier.'"

The Electric Archie

An example of Steve's electric guitar work, the electric "archie" is a modified version of the arch-top guitar first created in the early 1900s. The guitar has been left at full thickness to allow for greater presence with its Seymour Duncan Antiquity Humbucker Pickups which give this instrument the fat bottom end and thrum of more modern looking electric guitars. They are complemented by tonal controls and a three way switch to rotate between pickup selections. Other amenities include a nickel plated tailpiece, a signature feature on arch-top models in the1930s, tortoise pickguard, and Waverly tuners.

What is a Pickup?

A pickup acts as a transducer that captures mechanical vibrations, usually from stringed instruments and converts them into electrical signals which can then be converted (through amplification) into sound and recorded. Essentially cable is wrapped around a coil, when the instrument only has one coil the pickup is referred to as a single coil pickup, when two coils are combined it is often referred to as a "humbucker" pickup. The problem with single coil pickups (most often seen in Fender guitar models) is that they maintain a hum when in use. The resulting harmonics can affect an electric guitar's sound and may be undesirable to some musicians. To overcome this, the double-coil or humbucker was developed.

Techo-babble Alert

All the coils of the humbucker are wound reverse to one another. The sine wave signals in each pickup, created by the electro-magnetic interference, are equal, and are 180 degrees out of phase to one another. This is due to the reverse winding of the pickup coils. This leads to the two signals canceling each other once they meet on the signal path. However, the signal from the guitar string is doubled, due to the phase reversal caused by the out of phase magnets. The magnets being out of phase in conjunction with the coil windings being out of phase, put the guitar string signal from each pickup in phase with one another. When the two in phase guitar string sine wave signals meet, the amplitude of the wave doubles, and doubles the signal strength.

One side-effect of this technique is that when wired in series, as is most common, the overall inductance of the pickup is increased, which lowers its resonance frequency and attenuates the higher frequencies, giving a fatter and less trebly tone than either of the two component single-coil pickups would give alone. A second side-effect of the technique is that, because the two coils are wired in series, the resulting signal that is output by the pickup is larger in amplitude, thus more able to overdrive the early stages of the amplifier. This is the essence of the "humbucker tone."

Above: Crosby, Stills, Nash
& Young Perform at the 2006
'Freedom of Speech Tour'

Founded in 1956 by founding and current chairman Shiro Arai, Aria Guitars is based exclusively out of several cities in Japan with affiliates in the United Kingdom. Arai began with classical guitars, importing them as he was unable to purchase instruments in native Japanese music stores. Still a young man, the avid guitar player and instructor sought to purchase these instruments for his students and himself, but as demand for the classical instruments in the flamenco and nylon styles of Spain increased, Arai saw an opportunity and Aria was born. Business was a struggle at first and the company had to sell woolen goods to stay afloat, but slowly Aria began to gain a foothold. They began importing Fender guitars and amplifiers in the early 1950s just as rock 'n roll was taking off around the world. The Japanese market was largely unprepared for the level of demand that the burgeoning musical style would create for the electric guitar.

Aria began creating their own electric instruments in 1963. Since their inception, Aria's electric guitar lines have been trying to ride the popularity of musical movements within rock 'n roll with varying degrees of success. As a result the breadth of Aria's model range from semi-acoustic hollow bodies to the virtuoso guitars inspired by hard rocking solo masters, and even an electric upright bass. Today Aria continues to work toward being at the forefront of Japanese guitar making though continues to see difficulty in breaking into the mainstream of American musical thought.

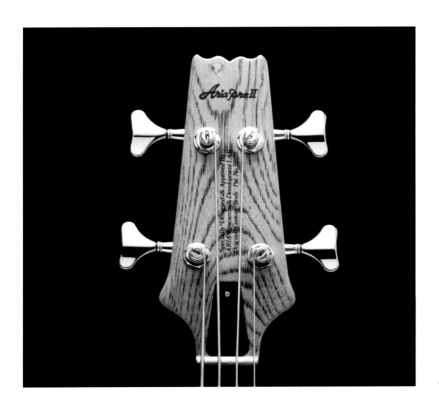

Intriguing Aria Designs

The XX-1 is an Aria design born out of their heavy metal days. The electric guitar sports a sharp cutting V body design, similar to the flying V shapes of Washburn and Gibson with in-house designed MH-1F, and MH-1R humbucking pickups. Its body is built from alder, with maple for its neck and traditional rosewood for its fingerboard. A feature common on more modern electric designs (and included here) is the locking tremolo. The locking tremolo was invented by Floyd D. Rose in 1979. The locking trem became highly popular among 1980s heavy metal guitarists due to its extremely wide range of variation and tuning stability. The original Floyd Rose system was similar to the Fender synchronized tremolo, but with a number of extra mechanisms. The first to be added and most obvious is a locking plate on the head nut, tightened with a hex key to fix the strings at this point after tuning. This provides extra tuning stability, particularly during use of the tremolo arm, which leads to the invention's only drawback – its prevention of adjustment of the pitch using the machine heads once the tremolo has been locked.

Another eerily similar body style is the PE-DLX2, which bears a striking resemblance to the Gibson Les Paul. This has been a trend among Japanese companies since the boom of the electric guitar in the 1950s. The copying of signature body styles actually lead to lawsuits headed by American companies fed up with Japanese guitar manufacturers who would not back down from their illegal practices. The PE-DLX2 is equipped with Duncan (not Seymour) designed H-103 humbucking pickups, and parts ways from the Les Paul inspired body design with an Aria specific tailpiece.

Left: the popular Aria models, the ZZ2 and SB100ri. Opposite page: a closer look at the SB100ri

Austin

Austin guitars is a company whose ethos is centered around the traditional elements that created the electric guitar, building models that have caught the eye of jazz and country musicians since its creation. The company also creates a full line of acoustic guitars, bluegrass instruments such as banjos and mandolins as well as amplifiers.

The Thunder Rock

Looking like a close cousin to the Gibson model SG, the Thunder Rock carries dual humbucking pickups that give the guitar a wide range of tones, from warm and smooth to bright, cutting rock 'n roll leads. Individually adjustable bridge saddles ensure precise harmonic tuning. In addition, stop-tailpiece provides better sustain, as well as aides in the ease of changing strings. Die-cast tuning machines with 14:1 ratio provide smooth, accurate tuning. Hardware for the Thunder Rock is triple chrome plating.

A Note on Body Styles

Throughout this history we will notice a certain ubiquitous nature of certain body styles. These seem to be those produced by Fender and Gibson chiefly those of the Fender Stratocaster and Telecaster, and the Gibson Les Paul, and SG. These body styles are instantly recognizable to nearly all guitar players across the globe and many non-musicians for their popularity. Whereas with the acoustic guitar is dependent on body style to produce much of its sound, the electric is not similarly bound, leaving the luthier or designer near complete freedom in creating shape. All that must be left is sufficient room to include the electronic components, which are getting smaller and easier to integrate every year. What will be interesting to see, as time progresses, is if the companies that have pioneered these signature body designs will consider their use by others a type of homage, as they have with American companies like Austin, or if they will consider it theft of intellectual property as they did once with the Ibanez guitar company, who were taken to court over the issue.

The Rock Standard

A more proprietary design from Austin features an arch-top body made from contoured ash. A Tune-a-Matic bridge is employed along with chrome plated hardware and die-cast tuners. Design of the headstock allows the strings to run straight from the nut to the tuning machine. This gives the string the maximum amount of downward tension that adds to the overall sustain (resonance of sound) of the instrument. The pearl inlaid logo enhances the overall appearance of the instrument, and adds notes of elegance. As has been the trend since its invention, dual humbucking pickups are used in the Rock Standard to give the electric the feel of a true belting instrument, a deep bass and even treble cut. The finish is sleeker, appears more modern than the vintage appeal of the SG-inspired Thunder Rock. This element differs from the norm of Austin's guitar lines which appear to mimic Fender and Gibson body styles across the board with certain exceptions in hardware, headstock, and feel. It is further evidence of just how iconic these guitar companies have been by the infusion of their styles into so many other guitar companies. They are nearly unavoidable.

Left: the AU792.
Opposite page: the AU792 in a variety of finishes; BU, CS and PR

B.C. Rich

Unlikely pairings have been the calling card of the B.C Rich guitar company since its creation. What would become one the most distinctive voices in the area of electric guitar creation began with its flamenco playing founder, Bernardo Chavez Rico. He built similar style guitars in his shop in Los Angeles for many years before building his first electric guitar in 1969. The first original B.C Rich guitar design was the Seagull, built in 1972. It featured a neck-through design which would become a distinctive feature for future B.C Rich designs as well as a lack of a "hell" or rounded bottom. By the close of the 1970s, Bernardo or "Bernie" as he was known, had gathered talented designers to go along with his team of able craftsman and set about building electric instruments totally unique from the standards of Fender and Gibson. The innovative designs of the Mockingbird, the Eagle, and late in the decade, the Bich, caught the eye of music's most nimble guitar players.

As their popularity grew, Rico recognized the need for a mass-produced B.C Rich guitar that could be delivered to the masses. The powerhouse that was/is Japanese production would come into play with the company founding the B.C Rico brand which would set apart guitars built overseas at a lower production cost. Rico Reed promptly sued B.C Rich over the use of their similar sounding name, and only a small number of Rico guitars ever made it into the United States.

Hair Metal and the Warlock

The B.C Rich Warlock is one of the defining body styles of the guitar company. Its shape is aggressive, angular, and all but instantly took to the hair metal community in the 1980s. Its dual Rich designed humbucking pickups gave it the raw, throaty sound that would otherwise be sorely lacking in the day's more well-quaffed acts. The 24 fret neck is also longer than the standard 22 which allows for higher notes and extended lead guitar play which was the hallmark of the hair metal "movement."

The body of the Warlock is built from agathis wood, the fretboard is made from rosewood and the neck is crafted from maple. Its look and feel are symptomatic of the entire B.C Rich line going forward since its headlong dive into the electric guitar arena. This company evokes the image of the guitar player as gunslinger (indeed they have a model after the same name), as lone man culling a crowd of thousands with expert technique and distorted reverb. It is at once an evocation as primal as the desire to win, as it is a desire to create that which was not there before. For B.C Rich the guitar, as they have shaped it in its electric form is quite literally a primal force, a weapon, an "axe."

Heavy Metal guitar players still flock to B.C Rich, even after largely leaving the hairspray behind. Bands like Slayer, Five Finger Death Punch, Motorhead, and The Sword among many other of Metal's finest proudly call B.C Rich home.

Right: Kerry King of Slayer performing at Download Festival Left: (red) the B C Rich Black Widow Bass, and Ignitor Model (black) and one of the earliest BC Rich models (yellow)

Behringer was founded in Germany in 1989 and has quickly grown into one of the largest designers and manufacturers of musical instruments and sound amplification. The company has a business presence in 10 countries around the world and when coupled with its intricate distribution network allows Behringer products to be sold in more than 125 countries. The strength of the company has been its technological advances in the world of audio which has then lead to attention in the musical instrument realm.

The USB Guitar

The melding of the computer as amplifier and sound modulator has long been experimented with by musicians and techs alike. Many of music's greatest hits and albums over the last ten years have been produced with equipment coming primarily from computer driven software like ProTools, Evanescence's debut album "Fallen" being a famous example of such equipment baring marketable fruit.

The Centari USB Guitar is one of Behringer's design attempts to meld the two pieces of equipment: musical instrument and computer. The electric guitar is designed to incorporate a USB cable to connect to a personal computer the same way it would normally connect to an amplifier. The computer serves as amplifier, recording system, and sound modulator allowing (through Behringer software) access to a number of tones, multi-tracks, and editing.

The Pros and the Cons

Benefits with this method include instant recording and the ability to manipulate sound as well as playability of what has been produced by the artist. The musician has complete control of the sound (tonality), and how accessible that sound is to others. The ability to create music and make that product instantly available (16 track recording in this case) to people in any location is something that has changed music in the modern era. No more will people wait for an album to come out or rush to the local music store to purchase it. Now, through the advent of digital media, downloading, iTunes and the like, consumers have an unprecedented ability to find the music they want and have nearly unlimited venues to purchase it.

On the surface the guitar appears constructed with traditional methods in mind: maple, solid body, 22-fret neck. However, much of the instrument's design is geared towards a virtual world, something for the studio and not the stage. Traditional musicians and set players have often overlooked these "New Age" style instruments for their lack of hardware integrity with their utilization of sub-standard pickups, tone woods, and tuners preferring to allow the computer to do the work. The tonal modulators that are employed by software such as Behringer's EnergyXT2.5 (works in PC or Mac), the recording software included with the Centari, have yet to replace traditional guitar amplifiers on stage in live performances.

As a company, Behringer's place is not unlike that of Japanese guitar companies that began producing their instruments at the dawn of rock 'n roll. They are creating a niche for themselves in the market by mining a largely untapped field, one that is devoid of the body style defining problems that face guitar companies competing with the likes of Fender and Gibson. Software may very well be the realm that defines how music is created going forward, and Behringer is already setting up to be ahead of the curve.

Benedetto

A native of the Bronx, Robert Benedetto was born into a family of artisan wood workers and musicians. That upbringing led Benedetto to create his first archtop guitar in 1968, and since that time has become one of the foremost luthiers to make guitars of that body style. His creations have been featured on many recordings, TV appearances and have also been housed in the Smithsonian Institute. In 1994, Benedetto (with his wife Cindy) published Making an Archtop Guitar, a seminal work in carrying the vintage construction methods of archtop guitars into the modern era. This publication, along with continued artist support for Benedetto-made guitars, landed the luthier a licensing agreement with Fender Musical Instruments in 1999, a partnership that would carry itself into the new millennium. Fender assured Benedetto that his guitars would continue to be produced in a small, supervised manufacturing workshop, and they were true to their word.

In 2006 the company joined forces with Howard Paul to begin producing a broader range of Benedetto instruments with affordability in mind. That company is currently located in Savannah, Georgia.

The Archtop Guitar in Brief

An archtop guitar is a steel-stringed, primarily acoustic or semi-acoustic guitar with a signature full body and concave (arched) top. The body design was one of the first to be modified for the electric guitar and was very popular with blues and jazz players of the early 1900s. Its invention is most often credited to Orville Gibson who patterned his archtop design after the popular designs of violins: each piece of the guitar was from a single piece of wood, thicker in the middle than at the sides. In a similar vein as Gibson, H.A Merrill also had an archtop design in the late 1800s/early 1900s based off of violin construction. His methods created an instrument that featured a metallic tailpiece and teardrop shaped "f-holes" that very much resembled archtop guitars that wouldn't become popular until Gibson began producing them in the 1930s.

The Benedetto Bravo and Deluxe

Produced in small workshops by skilled luthiers still overseen by Robert "Bob" Benedetto, the company's electric archtops are the standout of the production line. The Bravo features a thin body design and lightweight laminated spruce for its top with flamed maple back construction. Abalone floral inlay adorns the 12th fret of the electric guitar, which incorporates an in-house built Benedetto A-6 humbucking pickup. The Bravo Deluxe carries a body of chambered mahogany, and a top of select carved spruce. Warm, rich tone is carried through the instrument by expert electronics and twin A-6 humbuckers with a custom switching system to allow the guitar player more control over tone as well as volume.

As an independent company, Benedetto is a shining example of private luthiers flourishing in the growing corporate model of musical instrument sales. They have been able to keep their integrity intact and retain artistic control/vision with the man that founded them still overseeing a large portion of the custom work that is done at the workshop level. Where others have become disillusioned, Bob Benedetto has deepened resolve and listened to the players that love his instruments. What began as a husband and wide in a small shop in Florida in 1976 is now a well thought of organization.

*Left: Howard Aldern at the New
Orleans Jazz and Heritage Festival
Above: Randy Johnston at the PDX
Jazz Fesitval in 2009*

Bolin

Bolin Guitars was created in 1978 with the goal of building innovative guitars in both the electric and acoustic world. Today they sport a client roster which includes Billy F. Gibbons, Jimmy Page, Lou Reed, Albert King and many others. The company is still helmed by its founder John Bolin. It began as a small workshop and is now housed in a 6500+ square foot manufacturing facility. This has signaled a move away from the exclusive custom guitar work that had made Bolin into a popular name with musicians and to one that allows Bolin to produce a lower cost model for the everyday guitar player while still keeping its facilities owned and operated locally.

Custom work is still the strength of Bolin Guitars by far and an area that has allowed many other guitar companies to keep their instruments in the hands of popular musicians and thus generate revenues for their other product lines and lower end guitars. Bolin has worked with many artists to produce custom instruments for them that both give the musician control over the sound they're looking for as well as the body style. Bolin, like B.C Rich, stand as one the great modern innovators of the electric guitar in the area of body design.

The Bolin Custom Guitars

Bolin produces two lines of production instruments in the Bolin NS Guitar and Bass and the Bolin Classic. While these lines are very successful, Bolin is best known for its custom guitar work, which is why they were approached to create a custom instrument to commemorate the 40th anniversary of the Shelby Cobra. Bolin incorporated unique features that other luthiers (more tradition bound) seemed to ignore such as aluminum binding and inlay. Bolin is currently producing the Shelby electric guitar in an extremely limited run. These touches best evoked the spirit of the Shelby Cobra and cemented for an outside industry (car manufacturing) what other guitar companies have known for many years. Bolin has garnered the reputation as a guitar builder that will always think outside of the guitar body. It is no strange occurrence for guitars lined in fur, neon, and knives to come out of the Bolin Custom Guitar Shop.

Harley Davidson picked up where the Shelby Cobra left off and have recently announced a partnership with Bolin Guitars. The "Full Throttle Rock 'n Roll" is a collaborative festival spearheaded by the two companies to bring music, art, and motorcycles together in one place. Harley has encouraged and even commissioned local artists to create original artwork to advertise the festival in the continuing meld that is the guitar as a piece of art in addition to its aural appeal. The electric guitar is able to reach across lines of interest in a way that its predecessor the acoustic guitar has not in that the electric guitar has seemingly grown up with its fans since its rise coincides with the flowering of rock 'n roll, the tumultuous days of the 1960s and America's own love of the automobile.

Breedlove

Breedlove Guitar Co. is currently located in Bend, Oregon where it produces some of the world's finest guitars using exotic and experimental tone woods and electronics. Breedlove was started in 1974 by then surfer Kim Breedlove, who decided to make a living designing guitars and other stringed instruments while on a trip to Mexico. He began to educate himself on the finer points of crafting quality guitars and soon became quite the accomplished luthier. Though Kim is the creative thrust behind Breedlove Guitars the company itself was birthed by his brother Larry Breedlove and friend Steve Henderson, who partnered up and started the legitimate company in 1990. Kim Breedlove still works for the guitar builder as a master luthier.

In their inception Breedlove was a very traditional guitar building company, creating instruments that were acoustic in nature and geared toward the fingerstyle guitar player. Breedlove used woods naturally occurring in and around the company's home base in Oregon seeking to push the envelope in creating instruments of the highest quality. The differences came quickly as the company looked to create unique body styles for their instruments and rapidly began to branch out into the electric guitar side of the industry. Electronic systems were developed for Breedlove acoustics and electric guitars in a continuing trend of guitar companies seeking to keep control over the entire instrument in-house.

Breedlove Synergy System

Players are now able to create an electronic platform for their Breedlove acoustics and mandolins using the company's synergy system. Features include a custom installed pickup system from RMC, stout stage and studio able 15 foot 8-pin din connector, the RMC Polydrive II preamp equalizer and synthesizer blender with 13 pin connections, patch changes, and volume control. This system is now provided stock with select guitars of Breedlove's Atlas series. The versatility created using such an electronics package is a necessity for the modern, stage-minded guitar player.

Breedlove guitars also employ very modern technology coupled with their traditional hands-on luthiering approach. The Polhemus FastSCAN Cobra is one device that allows the guitar's individual parts to be scanned in a mesh format then saved to a computer as data files where they will be used to cut parts to the exact dimensions the original luthier built them to. This slices the time of a job that would normally take days into one that requires only hours to complete.

Breedlove Electric Guitars

The Mark I Chambered Electric Guitar is a perfect example of Breedlove's attention to detail and advanced work with electronics. Created to be lightweight and responsive, the Mark I features an asymmetrical mahogany body, with a carved top of either redwood or maple. Their signature headstock is fitted with Gotoh 510 tuners, and ebony peg overlay. Lollar and Seymour Duncan pickups are employed to give the Mark I the tone that would belie its slight frame. The guitar has also been ergonomically designed to cut down on the strain performers might feel from a long set or extended periods of playing. Breedlove provides excellent custom shop work as many of its guitars are built to the guitar player's exact specifications.

Brian Moore

Another young guitar company, Brian Moore Guitars was founded in 1992 by Patrick Cummings, Brian Moore, and Kevin Kalagher. Moore first met Cummings a year earlier while he was employed as an assistant to Ned Steinberger of Steinberger Sound. Cummings was working for Gibson at the time as a general manager of several divisions within the company, which included Steinberger. Moore was not a guitar player whose education centered primarily on furniture design and had come to Steinberger to increase his manufacturing and engineering knowledge. Patrick Cummings was a serious musician, with a background in Electrical Engineering and Business Management.

The third piece to this puzzle arrived in the same year, 1991, when Cummings came to know Kevin Kalagher, a businessman and avid guitar collector. Kalagher owned a successful commercial business in Connecticut and was doing print work for Steinberger Sound. After several projects, Kalagher approached Gibson about buying the Steinberger division. Gibson, expectantly, was not interested. Later, when Gibson decided to move Steinberger from New York to Nashville, Brian Moore decided not to follow the company. He approached his friend Patrick about a design concept for a guitar. After a meeting with now mutual friend Kalagher, the three men agreed on a business plan, and Brian Moore guitars was born (as a concept) with the idea of experimenting with composite materials to design the next great electric guitar.

As with other small shops, Brian Moore Guitars was initially conceived as a high-end custom guitar company with Kevin Kalagher pushing Moore and Cummings to design an elite class of instrument. The company was officially launched at the NAMM show in 1994 with Cummings and company garnering enough interest to land several distribution deals.

The iGuitar 2000

More affordable instruments are often required for a small shop to stay competitive with other guitar companies that sport foreign manufacturing facilities and wider networks of distribution. Brian Moore as a company began looking into the Korean manufacturing market as well researching their updated production methods in order to create more affordable versions of their custom shop models. The development of this instrument was driven by Patrick Cummings who had a singular vision for the most affordable

"technology based" guitar on the market. He loved the name "iGuitar" so he filed for a trademark, which they received in the USA, Japan, and other countries.

The i1 model electric guitar is based on Brian Moore's first guitar model the MC/1 but is an all-wood neck-through design, 22 fret, with tremolo and ivoroid binding and gold hardware. All iGuitar design models include featured on Brian Moore's custom shop models such as their comfort-contoured top and sculpted headstock with rear output jack. The iGuitar is also displays a 13-pin RMC system for fast tracking access to Roland guitar processors and other digital guitar products. Brian Moore has done something very similar to what Behringer Guitars is also attempting in that they are eagerly mining the melding of guitar as instrument with guitar the machine. A major advantage of these instruments is, while the parts are built overseas, each guitar is assembled, inspected, and shipped from their Brewster, New York facility.

Avid Brian Moore players Phil Campbell (above, top), John Abercrombie (above, bottom), and Phil Campbell performing in Sheffield (right)

Dave Bunker is a native of Washington State and has called it home for more than 35 years. He built the first Bunker Touch Guitar in 1961 with his father. It is the second patented stringed instrument in the United States. The instrument is unique in that it is constructed with two necks, one suited best for playing lead, and the other for playing Bass. Bunker constructed the instrument to highlight the "tapping" technique of guitar playing, a style which would later be modified and made famous by guitarist Eddie Van Halen (see: Eruption). The Touch Guitar uses this technique to play both necks at the same time with the strings being touched or tapped instead of plucked.

He unveiled the Touch Guitar to the American public on the ABC show "Ranch Party," a program being hosted at the time by Eddy Arnold, who quickly became infatuated with the unusual looking electric guitar. Bunker later played his invention in 1989 on "The Ralph Emery Show" in Nashville, Tennessee. The design has been constantly updated as new technologies have been developed and has been dubbed by Bunker as the "new musical instrument for the 21st century."

Bunker Electric Guitars

Outside of the Touch Guitar, Bunker has also built a successful wing of electric and acoustic guitars as well as basses. Dave Bunker is an accomplished luthier (in addition to being a longtime Las Vegas performer) and his talents are displayed most admirably in his MVP line of electric guitars. This electric is built with a deep, arched one inch exotic quilt maple top with recessed volume and tone controls with hum taps and pickup selector. Dense alder back is pocketed neck to rear pickup for semi hollow tone enhancement. Its composition is from the finest blocks of tone woods: alder from North America, maple, and premium grades of rare ebony.

The electronics for the MVP Bunker series are bolstered by the Bunker Magnum single string humbuckers with each string having its own preamp control. Other electronics are available per the musician's choice and depth of pockets. Bunker has also patented the "Top Load" bridge which is built into the MVP with Bell Brass intonators plated in either gold or chrome and is six-way adjustable.

Electronic Advancements

Whereas the acoustic guitar has been the province of the traditionalist, those seeking to preserve the old ways of guitar construction, the electric guitar as an instrument is a history that is still being written. Never has an instrument been so embraced by the march of electronic advancement as has the electric guitar. With the dawn of amplification and the pickup system came greater experiments in tone, not so much from the wood that is used to construct the guitar (though it still plays an integral part), but from the coils, metals, and even placement of those parts in order to create tonality and sustain sound quality.

These electronics have lead to the wild experimentations we have seen with companies such as Bunker, B.C Rich and Bolin. What will be most intriguing for the electric guitar is how its path is viewed by the musicians that pick them up as many are just as traditional as the first archtop guitars built in the 1900s are. Change happens at the speed of the luthier's thought and desire to build an instrument; acceptance will take more time.

Left: the Bunker Bass

Burns

James Burns has been called the "British Leo Fender" for the many parallels that have been drawn between the lives of the two. From the beginning, Burns preached development and refinement of his works in the field of guitar building in order to best reach that ideal instrument. Though there is much debate as to which luthier first invented which innovation there are many which are attributed to Burns, including the heel-less, glued-in neck; the 24-fret fingerboard; knife-edge bearing vibrato unit; active electronics; and stacked-coil pickups. Burns created guitar body styles that were somewhat inspired by Leo Fender's designs such as the Marvin, an unconventional take on the Stratocaster, and the Bison which combined fewer Fender influences with a shorter scale length and now classic "Wild Dog" electronics, which allowed for its high output Tri-Sonic pickups to be selected in many different combinations.

Burns (the company deeply in debt) was taken over by Baldwin in 1965, and as with other companies bought by the corporate giant, saw a period of decline shortly thereafter. Baldwin purchased the struggling company James Burns had founded for $380,000, a pittance compared to the $13 million CBS (who outbid Baldwin) paid for Leo Fender's company. It was nearly 20 years until Burns' designs saw the light of day and were given proper credit for their appeal and innovation. Burns Guitars were resurrected in 1992 and has been operated since that time as Burns London and is headed by Barry Gibson (no relation to the American guitar juggernaut) who employed Burns as a consultant. They are a dedicated team and have taken a nod to conservation, purchasing all of their British beech and sycamore from sawmills that support the Timber Trust Federation Forests Forever campaign. James Burns passed on in 1998 without seeing his company regain much of its former popularity.

The Bison 62

This model is the reissue of the original Bison, which was first created in 1962. It celebrates the 40th anniversary of the classic Burns body design with its inwardly curved body horns and advanced pickup selection system. This electric guitar features Burns exclusive batwing headstock and provides vintage tone and punch. The Wild Dog electronics and Split Sound settings remain intact. Amenities include: one tone control, one master volume, A/B pickup selector, three Burns Tri-Sonic pickups, Burns deluxe tremolo unit, Indonesian nato body, Bi-flex two way type truss rod, rosewood fingerboard and deluxe machine heads.

Musicians have an affinity for Burns guitars due to their signature look and sound. Much of the company's earlier success and popularity may have been due to the high tariffs that were in place in the 1960s, making it difficult for American made guitars to work their way into Britain. Burns guitars happily filled the vacuum created by such a vacancy. Burns has also worked with many famous guitar players including Brian May (Queen) for whom they produced a copy of May's famous Red Special guitar, which uses Burns Tri-Sonic pickups. That model was awarded "Best Guitar of the Year" by Guitarist Magazine in 2001.

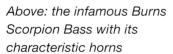

Above: the infamous Burns Scorpion Bass with its characteristic horns

Carvin

Carvin has been a builder of electric and acoustic guitars as well as amplifiers and other premium audio products for more than 60 years. Similar to other companies in the recent past Carvin has begun to delve into the digital applications of the electric guitar with production of MIDI synth access guitars. Carvin is based out of the United States and still creates the majority of their products within its borders.

Lowell Kiesel founded the company in 1946 under the name L.C Kiesel Company in Los Angeles, California. After a brief stay in the founder's home state of Nebraska, the company returned to L.A under the new name in 1949, Carvin, a name he chose for his two eldest sons, Carson and Gavin. The first products produced by the new Carvin were guitar pickups, which then led to amplifiers, guitars, basses and other equipment. As the 1950s rolled on, Carvin had yet to really head its own design team, building guitars from Hofner components and acting as a reseller of some Fender and Martin guitars, though this would change as the 1970s approached.

By that decade Carvin had created its own design team with an eye set to producing its own unique instruments. Their first move was to create a custom guitar shop that belied the size of Carvin, which already boasted large manufacturing facilities. Carvin gained notoriety in the industry in the 1980s as many other companies had by attaching their name to popular musicians such as Frank Zappa, The Eagles, and Steve Vai. They were also one of the first companies to embrace MTV as a marketing tool for their instruments. The 1980s also signaled a shift by Carvin away from the set-neck guitar designs to a neck-through body design.

Neck-Through Design vs. Set-Neck Models

Neck-through body design means that essentially the neck of the guitar extends the entire way through the body of the guitar as opposed to being bolted (bolt-on) or glued (set-neck) into/onto the body. Neck-through design creates a much greater stability in the electric guitar, which often takes more punishment than its acoustic counterparts. It also provides for better sustain of vibration throughout the instrument as the guitar is one piece, not individual parts which are vibrating and, under enough stress, could potentially come apart as some mass-produced instruments have in the past. The set-neck design is still very popular, however, and is used by many elite guitar companies such as Gibson and Paul Reed Smith.

Carvin Electric Guitars

Many of Carvin's models still emulate the body styles of guitar builders with a longer history of creative popular body styles. The CS3 California Single Cut Carved Top is an example of a Les Paul inspired model with some unique twists. The carved body is made entirely out of mahogany, which is unusual as most guitar builders use a separate wood for the guitar's top, back, and sides. Finish is applied to the entire guitar to give a sleek, showroom style appearance that allows its simplistic lines to look like a classic. A set-in neck is employed with its headstock emblazoned with a 24k gold Carvin logo. C22J and C22B classic humbuckers and Sperzel locking tuners give the CS3 that throaty Les Paul style sound and playability.

Left: the Vinny Vincent Invasion
Above: Jerry Jeff Walker and his
favorite Carvin guitar

Charvel

Wayne Charvel created a guitar repair business in Azusa, California, which he named after himself in the early 1970's. By the close of that decade, Wayne had sold the company to an employee of his called Grover Jackson. Wayne Charvel promptly left the company shortly thereafter and has had nothing to do with the business since that time.

Jackson set about building guitars of high quality right away under the Charvel name, and in the 1980s he was introduced to a young guitarist playing for Ozzy Osbourne, Randy Rhoads. Randy and Jackson began to design a guitar that featured an angular, neck-through body style that was inspired by Rhoads himself that would evolve into a model named the "Concorde." Jackson was worried about attaching the Charvel name to Rhoad's unorthodox guitar so he put his own last name on the headstock, thus launching the Jackson guitar brand. That electric guitar's name would later be changed to the "Rhoads" and it remains a top seller for Jackson to this day.

Grover sold Jackson/Charvel to Japanese manufacturer AMIC in 1989. Charvel guitars was moved in a production capacity abroad to Japan as a result of its purchase though interestingly enough its neck plates still bore the address of AMIC's Texas address as opposed to the island of Japan where they were actually made.

Tough Times and Popular Guitars

The 1990s proved to be a difficult time for Charvel. Whereas their active-electronics model electric guitars had been popular with metal guitar players in the late '80s, the grunge rock movement of the '90s proved the death knell of that period of musical decadence. The Charvel name was relegated to lower budget instruments, which caused popularity and quality of their product to plummet.

The Fender Musical Instruments Corporation bought Charvel and Jackson in 2002 and the guitar line experienced a rebirth of sorts as production was again returned to the United States in the form of custom guitars and signature models. The models were named after the location of the workshop

in which they were created, San Dimas. Charvel also created a line of Warren DeMartini signature and the all-new USA Production Model Series.

The San Dimas Style 2 2H

This American made Charvel model features a Fender Telecaster inspired Alder body, contoured back and 1-piece maple neck. Seymour Duncan JB and '59 humbucking pickups are used to give the 2H a sound that flies in the face of the cutting tone that guitar players have come to expect from the Telecaster body style. Patented Floyd Rose tremolo and Grover Mini Tuners add to the artisan feel of this handcrafted in the USA instrument.

Charvel is a perfect example of how modern musical movements have shaped the way guitars are built and received by the public. Just as arch top guitars rose to prominence on the wings of blues and jazz movements in the 1930s, Charvel originally climbed into the spotlight thanks to the fleet fingers of metal music's most inspired players in Randy Rhoads before being plowed under by the next reaper to take its place on top of the musical pile that was the Seattle, Washington based grunge music movement in the 1990s. In this business, the ability to adapt is the key.

Above: the Fifth Batch Family
Right: a closer look at the So Cal in Ferrari Red

Bill Collings has had a lifelong love of the guitar and the craft that is building it. His life nearly took another path, as he did not decide to pursue his dream of becoming a luthier until he was knee deep in medical school. His interest in medicine diminished, Collings left school and moved to Texas in the 1970s and settled down in Houston. He spent the next few years there learning his craft as a trial and error process of building instruments and learning materials and electronics.

His next move was plotted for California where other great guitars have been built and flourished throughout the years. Bill only made it as far as Austin, where he met and shared workspace with fellow luthiers Tom Ellis and Mike Stevens. Bill would next set up his own workshop in a converted "one car" garage. He toiled long and hard and steadily garnered a reputation as a meticulous craftsman. By the close of the 1980s, Collings had entered a thousand square foot facility and was able to hire a staff.

The same years an order of 24 custom guitars aided Collings in stepping onto the national guitar scene. From there the ball was only increasing in speed as Bill upgraded to a 3200 square foot facility in 1992, and by 2005 the shop size had tripled and what began as a staff of only two had now increased to more than 50.

Collings Builds an Electric

After nearly 32 years building acoustic guitars, Bill Collings turned his eye to the electric guitar. Archtop guitars were built by Collings in the 1980s and expanded to mandolins by the close of the 1990s. His electric guitars were built with the same meticulous eye for detail that made Bill Collings a name as a master luthier decades earlier and quickly established their own bright reputation.

The I-35 Deluxe is built of a semi-hollow Honduran mahogany body and inset alder center block. Its fully carved top with F-holes complements a premium flame top. The woods are finished with rare East Indian rosewood fingerboard and ebony peg head veneer. Humbucking pickups designed by Jason Lollar are set beneath the I-35's strings with grained ivoroid at its top and back binding. This electric also incorporates 1950s style wiring into its electronics package in order to give it true vintage feel and tonal range.

The Trends in Modern Guitar Companies

Collings story of success is the result of hard work and dedication. His ability to steer his own ship whereas others wilted in the face of adversity and financial hardship is not unlike that of luthiers and craftsman that came before him. There are those that have been bought out by large corporations like Fender which was sold to media giant CBS or Gibson which was purchased by Baldwin only to then be bought back by dedicated investors and believers in the ideals that make music and musical instruments so compelling the world over, and there are those companies that have had one struggling independent owner working in small shops hoping to have the success of a luthier like Bill Collings. Where the guitar has flourished, it is under the stewardship of a fine craftsman dealing a product that they are passionate about.

Cort

The beginnings and development of Cort as a brand of electric guitars is laced with business decisions, imports, and venture capital. Jack Westheimer began setting up connections with Japanese guitar makers in the 1960s with the intention of importing Japanese made guitars into the United States. In 1973, he founded the Too-ah company in South Korea with business partner Yung H. Park. This company would eventually be called Cor-Tek, which was named after Westheimer's Cortez brand name. Park would eventually acquire the operations of Cor-Tek outright from Westheimer, and the company would become the manufacturer of the guitar brand known as Cort.

Cort lacks the signature guitar body style that has been so prevalent in American based guitar companies and they have sought to compensate for this by becoming the world's largest producer of guitars by variety. Cort claims to have a guitar to suit any guitar player's unique musical needs, and the numbers suggest that no other company has the production capacity or model output that Cort has.

Cort's production focus is not on Cort guitars specifically but more on contract jobs for other companies. Cort is the company most often contacted by other guitar makers when they are seeking to create more affordable versions of their domestically produced instruments. Parkwood, ESP, Schecter, and G&L are all companies that Cort has produced guitars for over the years.

A Full Breadth of Production Models

Cort's vast array of instruments is displayed most admirably in their electric guitar production runs. The company has been able to slide through body styles in ways that have been both the gift and curse (American guitar companies have brought several lawsuits against Asian guitar companies since the 1970s) of Asian guitar manufacturers since they began looking to the West for inspiration. The majority of its body styles appear as amalgams of the world's most loved electric guitars such as Gibson, Rickenbacker, and Fender.

The ELV-ZK has a close appearance to the Les Paul custom with its round bottom end and single cutaway. Its construction features a string-through design and set-in neck, mahogany body and ebony for its fingerboard. Amenities include twin EMG 81/60 Humbuckers, Die cast tuners, and 3-way pick-up selection. The X-6 SM produced by Cort has a body style that is similar to the electric guitars created by Ibanez and is built of American basswood. Its construction features a bolt-on neck, jumbo frets (2.9mm) with a lead guitar ringing 24-space fret length.

The strength from this method of guitar making is that Cort really has no expectations for its models. There is no "one look" for a Cort guitar and as such, the company is free to produce models using whatever electronic makeup, body style, wood choices and price range that it chooses. This versatility somewhat offsets the lack of signature models and body style recognition though these two factors have served many smaller, elite luthier workshops in the past. Cort has made up for quality with quantity and as such may have diminished the perception that the Asian market can be a place where a master luthier might flourish as larger corporations continue to gobble up smaller shops.

Right: Cort guitar fan, Larry Coryell

Crafter does not begin in a small workshop or large corporate manufacturing facility. In what might be the humblest beginning for a guitar company, Crafter began in the basement of HyunKwon Park's Korean home in 1972. Park began with three others producing classical guitars geared toward the Korean domestic market and his efforts quickly bore fruit with a good reputation for sound quality. The fledgling outfit sought out larger facilities than Park's home could afford and in 1978, they moved from Seoul to Yangju-gun.

During this time, Crafter's guitars were produced under the brand "Sungeum" which is Korean for "accomplishing the sound." The name, while still recognizable and highly regarded in Korea to this day, did not satisfy the international appeal that Park sought for his company. When InJae Park, the founder's eldest son, joined the company in 1986 he believed the name Sungeum (much as his father) was too difficult a word for the export market, so he created a new brand, one that would be both easy to remember and the conveyance for his new image. InJae chose the name Crafter. The guitar company is now registered in more than 40 countries throughout the world.

Under New Management

InJae's father, HyunKwon, remained as chairman of Crafter even as InJae took the company in a new creative direction. Their largest factory opened in 2000 and boasts some of the most modern amenities available in guitar making, a move that has been the earmark of Asian guitar makers moving forward into the 21st century. The numbers show the increase in productivity with their staff of just over 140 churning out more than 60,000 guitars in 2001 alone. As a result of their production capacity and speed, Crafter guitars are now sold in more than 30 countries with the United Kingdom receiving 10,000 units of the company's 2001 workload.

But the quantity produced is not the main objective. The emphasis is always to put care into the making of each guitar to produce the finest instruments. They are only released to players when the maker is sure that they are in the best condition and any that don't make the grade are broken up. InJae joining Crafter was a most significant step for the company because, like his father, he has a talent for designing good guitars and a love for building them. He has developed and designed many new models that are protected by patents in Europe and the USA. InJae Park believes that building instruments of the highest quality, of the best value, listening to the needs of the market and providing a continuous supply is the way to continue the progress and success that Crafter is enjoying throughout the world today.

Crafter Convoy SP/SBK Guitar

A gothic, flat black finish sets this Crafter electric apart from other models produced by the Korean instrument maker. Alnico pickups give it that malevolent thrum of true humbuckers that highlights Crafter's attention to quality as well as quantity, a direction that is a shift for the larger Asian manufacturers. Solid mahogany is used for the body, with maple for the neck. The set-neck construction allows Crafter to maintain low cost while attaining a moderate level of vibration threshold through the instrument.

Daisy Rock

Daisy Rock Guitars was created in 2000 by designer Tish Ciravolo with the intention of creating guitars specifically for girls. "As a longtime musician my experience has been that a guitar for girls is long overdue," writes the designer/founder. "Standard guitars are often too big and bulky for the young female form. When I first started playing bass as a teenager, the instrument felt like a bat in my female-sized hands. At times, I wanted to quit because I felt like maybe the instrument just wasn't for me or that I wasn't good enough to play it. I've encountered so many female musicians who have experienced the same set of feelings and I truly believe this is why we have a lack of female guitar-playing musicians in popular music."

Daisy Rock represents a departure from the male-centric world of the electric guitar and the blistering soloist or frontman that has come to be popular in modern rock 'n roll. They're here to prove women play just as well as men and should have guitars designed for them just as men do. "As the mother of two girls, part of my motive for creating the Daisy Rock is selfish," writes Ciravolo in the company's mission statement, "I want to be able to provide them with opportunities that I didn't have. If they want to pursue music, I want them to feel comfortable and capable. The Daisy Rock is a line of high-quality instruments that are attractive and are a perfect fit for girls. My hope is that they will help give them an opportunity to build their self-assurance through music."

Practicing What They Preach

The company in particular is working through charitable organizations to swing the pendulum to a more artist centric field and remove the masculine shadow over the craft of guitar making and marketing. Ciravolo has been aggressive in her strategy to get her company's message to the public and keep it in their consciousness. Daisy Rock as a company has had a presence at The Women's International Music Festival, sponsored the Bay Area Girls Rock Camp, The Southern Rock 'n Roll Girl's Camp, and the Girls Rock Vegas Day Camp, among many others.

The Rock Candy Custom Special

The Daisy Rock Custom Special Electric Guitar features a sycamore body with a contoured top and a set, 24-3/4"-scale mahogany neck. The neck construction increases the guitar's ability to sustain or vibrate and maintain that vibration. The 22-fret fingerboard is made of rosewood and inlayed with stars. Other features of this Rock Candy Series guitar include a TonePros Tune-o-matic-style bridge with string-through body, black hardware, and Duncan Designed active humbucker pickups. A push-pull tone control "taps" or splits the humbucker coils, adding to the sonic versatility with single-coil tones. Daisy has been able to enter the fray of the guitar industry and remain competitive by playing face-up with their constituents. Ciravolo and her design team have managed to create eye-catching, lightweight, competitively priced and sonically viable electric guitars geared to be the haven that female guitar players have lacked, a place to call their own.

Right: the Daisy Rock Heartbreaker model
Opposite page: a closer look at the Stardust Retro-H De-Luze model

Danelectro

Danelectro is a manufacturer of musical instruments and accessories, specializing in rock instruments such as guitars, bass guitars, amplifiers and effects units (a popular end of the company's production). Nathan Daniel founded the company in 1947, and throughout that time they produced amplifiers for Sears, Roebuck and Company as well as Montgomery Ward. As the 1950s got underway, Danelectro began creating its own line of solidbody electric guitars and amplifiers and also worked as a contract player creating guitars for various names, such as Silvertone and Airline. While they bared the Danelectro look and sound, they lacked the name.

Next came hollow-bodied guitars (constructed out of Masonite and plywood to save costs and increase production speed,) distinguished by Silvertone's maroon vinyl covering, Danelectro's light tweed covering, the concentric stacked tone/volume knobs used on the two-pickup models of both series, and the "lipstick-tube" pickups (invented by placing the entire mechanism into spare lipstick tubes), these lines aimed to produce no-frills guitars with good tone at low cost.

By 1956, Danelectro introduced the six-string electric bass, which would be adopted by other companies such as Fender with the Fender VI.

The six string bass never proved especially popular but found an enduring niche in Nashville as the instrument of choice for "tic-tac" bass lines. In 1966, Danelectro was sold to MCA. A year later, in 1967, the Coral line was introduced, known for its hollow-bodies and electric sitars. In 1969, the Danelectro plant was closed, due to MCA's attempt to market Danelectros to

small guitar shops rather than large department stores. As is often the case when larger companies overtake smaller shops, Danelectro was the victim of not being understood.

In the late 1990s, the Evets Corporation started selling primarily copies of old Silvertone and Danelectro guitars, newly designed effects pedals, and small amplifiers. After initially selling well, guitar sales slowed down to the point where Danelectro stopped posting sales after 2001, opting to concentrate on effects pedals. In 2006, the new owners of Evets decided on a new marketing model for the guitars, selling a limited number of guitars each year.

Danelectro has also been a voice for charity work, aiding such causes as the SJK Orphanage in Nairobi, Kenya. Through their efforts, the orphanage has been able to purchase two more acres of land, drill successful water wells that produce over 5000 liters per hour, run electric cables, bring in computers, and a few Danelectro electric guitars.

The Dead On '67

The "Dead-On '67" electric guitar from Danelectro is an authentic reissue of the 1967 Hornet with a satin finish, nickel hardware, a truss rod that adjusts at the headstock, the original swivel rosewood bridge that intonates, and souped-up lipstick pickups that are hum-canceling when both are on. The "Dead-On '67" guitar also features the original Danelectro vibrato and split pickguard.

The Dano 63

The Dano 63 is a remake of the original '63 electric guitar that launched a thousand garage bands and more than a few pro careers. The body construction is just like the original with a hardboard top and bottom laminated to a plywood frame. The hollow inner chamber produces the resonance that is part of Danelectro's unique tone. The '60s era lipstick pickups have been replicated to be hot, sweet, and to sound just right. The bridge and tuners are fully upgraded. Zero-gloss nickel hardware accents the appealing vintage palate.

Left: Led Zepplin's Jimmy Page and his Danelectro guitar
Below: a look at Jimmy Page's DC59

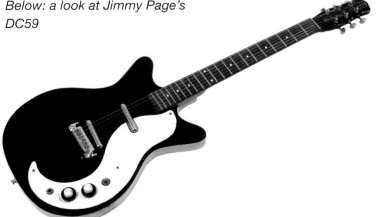

Dean is a rock 'n roll guitar company if there ever was one. Dean Guitars was created in 1976 by a 17-year-old named Dean Zelinsky, a luthier with strong connections to the rock 'n roll community and a desire to change the landscape of guitar design. Originally based in Chicago, Illinois, Dean has made a name for itself producing electric guitars that have caught the interest of the heavy metal and rock communities. Dave Mustaine (Metallica, Megadeth) and perhaps more famously the late "Dimebag" Darrell Abbott have ridden Dean electric guitars to great success. The vast majority of Dean's production runs have been allocated to the electric guitar and it has garnered a lasting reputation with hard rock and metal communities thanks to their signature body styles and commitment to expert craftsmanship. Dean Guitars is currently owned by Armadillo Enterprises, which also owns Luna Guitars.

In 1991, Dean Zelinsky sold his company to its present owner Armadillo Enterprises. In 2008 he removed himself altogether from the guitar company he created saying, "I can no longer attach my name to the reputation, quality and direction of Dean Guitars or its current objectives…I wanted to get back to what put Dean on the map originally—building high-quality instruments that shape both the image and tone of guitar players, from the beginner to world-class professionals." Later that same year Zelinsky announced in partnership with Jeff Diamant (Diamond Amplification) and Terry Martin, the creation of DBZ Guitars LLC, a guitar line that would be overseen and controlled directly by the luthier.

USA Razorback Tribute

"Dimebag" Darrell Abbott was the chugging, fleet-fingered power behind seminal metal band Pantera, and was struck down in a tragic moment as a fan rushed the stage and shot him as a member of Damage Plan in 2004. The USA Razorback is Dean's tribute to the fallen guitar hero and one that Abbott helped put on the rock map, and it was this model he was working on with Dean Zelinsky at the time of his passing. This electric guitar was hand built by Zelinsky for Dean and produced in a very limited run. A zebra Dimarzio and Seymour Duncan Dimebucker (designed with help from Abbott) provide the aural artillery for the razorback, which is not to mention the jagged edges that are incorporated into its body style that make this Dean model look and sound unique. It also incorporates a Floyd Rose locking tremolo, 12th fret razorblade inlay, which is a tribute in itself to Judas

Priest, one of Abbott's longtime favorite metal bands. Dean currently produces more than 30 electric guitar models in their "Dimebag Darrell" series.

The iconic status of "Dimebag" Darrell Abbot shows how the music industry and guitar players in general may be shaped by one man's mastery of the instrument. We will see this in Fender with the Stratocaster made legend by Jimi Hendrix and Eric Clapton, or even the Hofner Bass which would look bland had it not been in the hands of Paul McCartney. The relationship is very much a symbiotic one between workshops, players, and fans. Much like a live performance that, without crowd interaction and participation, it would just be another dial on the radio to change.

Above: Dave Mustaine of Megadeth
Opposite Page: Michael Shenker

DiPinto Guitars is a small family owned company operating out of Philadelphia, PA. Founded in 1995 as a repair shop, the store slowly evolved into a showroom specializing in oddball vintage guitars and Chris DiPinto's own guitar creations. Over the years, DiPinto has grown to include a full-scale guitar manufacturing operation while still operating the original retail outlet. In the early 1980s, well-sought-after session guitar player David Lindley began mining the discarded bins of imported and domestic guitars like Teiscos and Silvertones. Their unique tone instantly put a sonic signature on his music. DiPinto guitars of Philadelphia has designed models that straddle the line between classic American design and imported rarities.

Galaxie's 2 and 4

The radical design elements shared by the DiPinto Galaxie 4 and Galaxie 2 may require a certain pomp and pageantry on stage, but much of the guitars' strength is functional. The Galaxie 4 displays a matching tortoise pickguard and headstock ensemble, star inlays, and four pickups. But the angled headstock combines the look of a Fender with the ability of a Gibson to maintain tension across the 42mm nut without the use of string trees. This is especially functional on the Galaxie 4, where it helps the tremolo stay in tune.

These lightweight guitars display great balance with their neck built to hang ergonomically when the musician is in the standing position. The maple, four bolt necks are attached to the headstock with a luthiers' joint (bolt-on). The Galaxie 4's Jaguar style tremolo maintains the guitar's tuning, though there is some loss of sustain. The Galaxie 4 brings Fender to mind with a 25 1/2" scale length and a club-like shape to the neck. The Galaxie 2 nods to Gibson with its standard tune-o-matic bridge and stop tailpiece configuration.

The DiPinto Look and Sound

The four pickup set that has become the signature of DiPinto models is a departure from the norm of electric guitar design. The five-way switch offers bridge pickup alone, bridge and two adjacent pickups, middle two, all four or neck pickup alone. Positions 3 and 4 are hum-canceling combinations of the single coils.

These DiPinto designed pickups are powerful enough to let you lower the middle two a bit, if they get in the way of your picking, and still have plenty of punch. The bridge pickup provides a Strat-like cutting tone but also has enough midrange to perform well once the overdrive of an amplifier is kicked on. Position 2 offers a fine funk tone, and the neck pickup by itself gives enough warmth for jazz combined with punch enough for blues. The middle two together make a unique sound that will in future be known as "DiPinto Tone," like a Strat neck/middle combo but with more midrange tone.

The Silver Sparkle Galaxie 2 came with two humbuckers and a three-way switch. In all actuality, these humbuckers are made up of two single coils each, wired together in series and mounted separately. This allows the musician to shape their tone by raising or lowering half the pickup. The versatility created in these pickup mounts is the hallmark of the electric guitar's advantage upon creation. Even after market the guitar player has complete control over tone.

*Left: the Galaxie 4 model
Opposite page: a closer look
at the Belvedere Deluxe Bass*

This is a guitar company that consolidates many of the best features of different eras in guitar design. Dieter Goelsdorf's Duesenberg methods of guitar construction, features and sounds have written and in some cases painted the full array of color and sound of music since the 1900s. The art deco style design of headstock, pickguard and metal components gives Duesenberg its own eye-catching look, while the body design bases on the old traditional Jazz guitars like being built from the 1940s in Europe and in the USA.

These design elements are combined with the best possible electric guitar construction values of the 1950s: Grand Vintage Alnico pickups, classical Fender scale length plus a Gibson-like fingerboard radius. Most of the vintage-style tailpieces, bridges, tremolos, pickups and controls come with greatly improved details. Duesenberg has taken the innovations of others and used them to create something stylistically different and sonically relevant.

A History of Duesenberg

Duesenberg Guitars is a German company producing high-end electric guitars and basses with a distinctive Art Deco design since 1986. The company's name alludes to the legendary car company Duesenberg. All models are built in the Duesenberg factory in Hannover; all hardware, including the single-coil/vintage, P-90 and humbucking pickups are designed in-house.

The electric guitars feature solid and semi-solid, 12 and 6 string models. The range also includes signature models for German guitarist Carl Carlton, Ron Wood (Rolling Stones) and Mike Campbell (of Tom Petty's Heartbreakers); a custom "49er" was built for Keith Richards. The latest version of the Starplayer TV incorporates Duesenberg's version of the Piezo Bridge. In addition, the company has designed a range of replacement bridge/vibrato units. These include: one based on the famous Bigsby vibrato and incorporates a novel-locking device, while another is a bolt-on version of the B-Bender. The lightweight plus comfortable position of controls of these stage and studio guitars provide a distinctive playing performance for the most demanding player.

Latest Models from Germany

The new 49er guitar has been built to take center stage with some of the great guitars from the early '50s. Duesenberg's goal was to build a guitar that would meet the company's already high expectations and yet feel right at home in the hands of accomplished guitar players throughout the world.

The combination of engineering and wood selection along with Duesenberg DP90 pick-ups has allowed the new 49er to join the other unrivaled guitars found in the Duesenberg line. With an arched maple top and the fine lines created by the light mahogany body conjures vintage look with modern playability. Its string-through design and jumbo frets add features which guitar players have long sought after from a guitar so light and easily carried while on stage. The 49er truly combines Gibson body style and tone with Fender's playability. A fine line to ride but one that Duesenberg has done well.

Above: Mike Campbell
Right: Joe Walsh plays with the Eagles in Concert

Dunn

In 1966, Michael began a three-year apprenticeship in guitar making under luthiers Jose Orti and Jose Ferrer, at George Bowden's workshop in Palma de Mallorca, Spain. Both Orti and Ferrer were members of families with a long-standing history in instrument making. They taught him the traditional Spanish artisan's methods of classical and flamenco guitar construction. Dunn would revive the Selmer/Macafferri style of guitars in North America almost singlehandedly. He became an influential teacher himself whose students were the likes of master luthiers such as Shelley Park and Chuck Shifflett.

As a guitarist fascinated by the acoustic jazz of Django Reinhardt's "Hot Club de France" quintet, Michael developed an interest in the Maccaferri guitar and the technology of the interior soundbox-reflector. His aim was to maximize the sound-projection abilities of the instrument while preserving its authentic "Django" tone. He constructed his guitars to be balanced and responsive. The personal touch and technique of the player determine the sound of the instrument, because an instrument built with quality in mind responds in different ways in the hands of different players.

The Fallacy of Handmade Guitars

In the modern era, the term "handmade" is applied, as often as not, to guitars produced by a sizable workforce assembling identical parts made by computer-controlled machinery. Such advancements have allowed these factories to reduce errors in construction and give an instrument its "handmade" feel but are not true to the spirit of that craftsmanship. Dunn tunes an individual soundboard and selects all its adjacent components to match that tuning. Hence, no two instruments are exactly alike. Maximum output from any given set of parts, personally selected, assembled and tuned is what Dunn strives for, not standardization. While this lifts the ceiling on quality it also opens the door to the basement.

Dunn shapes each guitar by hand without the use of form, that is to say a template. The Vancouver, BC, luthier's success built steadily over the course of 30 years and when George Gruhn saw Dunn's work at a trade show in the mid-'90s, the Nashville retailer promptly commissioned a Dunn gypsy jazz guitar for immediate delivery. As legend has it, the first customer to play that guitar bought it, a certain guitar legend named Chet Atkins, who kept it until his passing.

Current Dunn Models

Many of Dunn's guitars are the perfect example of hybrid design, which combines elements of several of his current models. Crafted in the style of the Selmer "Petit Bouche," the favored model of Django himself, the guitar features the small oval soundhole in a top made of solid book matched cedar of exceptionally fine grain. This design is notable for its projection and punch and is favored by many lead players in the Manouche style. The sides are bent from solid rosewood, and the back has been crafted from rosewood with an inset of purpleheart in the style of the Dunn Belleville model.

From the Stardust model, the guitar features a faster 25.4" scale, the modern standard for most acoustic archtop and dreadnought guitars. The neck is lightened with the addition of a slotted peghead, standard on the vintage Selmers and an option on Michael's Mystery Pacific and Daphne models. Finally the peghead is graced with a smooth set of genuine gold Waverly tuners. The neck is wide, flat, and fast, with a fingerboard width of 1 13/16" at the nut, which is scalloped by hand. The French polished top is protected with a pair of flamenco-style clear plastic scratch plates.

Eastwood

Eastwood Guitars calls Ontario, Canada home. The company's history, however, is something that is distinctly out of the United States. Founder Mike Robinson, a guitar player with discerning if not eccentric taste whose first instrument was a '70s Japanese El Degas SG copy, did indeed have rock star dreams. Immediate success came from another avenue as Robinson made a successful foray into the high-tech business, but after relocating to Silicon Valley from Toronto in 1991, his interest in "off-the-beaten-path" guitars was reignited by frequent visits to Guitar Showcase in San Jose. All was a pipe dream until Robinson saw an opportunity that arrived with the "dot-com era" of business and one that incorporated his technological savvy all too well. Robinson began buying and selling guitars, ultimately launching myrareguitars.com in the late 1990s to help other enthusiasts identity their EKOs, Teiscos, Voxes, and other rare and vintage department store style guitars.

The Appeal of New-Age Vintage

In 2001, Robinson procured a 1987 "new old stock" Mosrite and the idea began to seriously germinate that marketing vintage replicas would be both feasible and profitable. His goals were simple. He wanted guitars that could actually be played rather than locked away as fragile investments, and offered better construction and easier playability than that of the quirky originals. Lastly, and perhaps most importantly, he wanted his guitars sold at affordable prices.

His first attempt involved reselling Italian EKO guitars, but soon Robinson decided to leap into the game himself and manufacture remakes initially culled from his own collection of vintage and sometimes outlandishly styled guitars. He went to NAMM, met with Chinese and Korean distributors, and placed orders. When asked for his company name, Robinson remembered watching a Clint Eastwood movie the previous night, and blurted out, "Eastwood."

Current Eastwood Developments

Based in Canada since 2002, Eastwood currently offers 20 guitar models (including the just-released replica of the Airline Town & Country played by Jack White in the Raconteurs) and three basses in colors ranging from red to greenburst to sunburst to transparent amber and beyond, depending on the model. Keeping the Eastwood replicas mass-production friendly and affordable has necessitated some detours from

the original designs. For example, gone are the fiberglass bodies of the Airlines and the aluminum necks of the Wandres. Still, the majority of Eastwood's released replicas clock in at just over a grand, which is still pricy for the younger musician.

A Guitar Company for the Fans

The Airline '59 2P is Eastwood's remake of an electric guitar that was produced by VALCO for Montgomery Ward in 1958-1968. White Stripes/The Raconteurs/The Dead Weather member Jack White has popularized this model which features chambered mahogany for its body, rosewood fingerboard, and maple neck. Its electronics sport two Airline vintage single coil pickups, 3-way vintage switch plate, Tune-O-Matic custom chrome Tail Bridge, and is plated in nickel and chrome. The model shows Robinson's commitment to producing instruments that are true to the original intentions of the maker as well as keeping them economical. Eastwood is a guitar company created by a fan, a man that wanted to bring his vintage collections to life.

Above: (from top), the Airline '59 Town and Country, Airline Lap Steel and Wandre DLX
Right: a closer look at the Messanger model

Eko is the firm founded by Oliviero Pigini in 1959 and was the largest musical instruments firm in Europe from 1964 until the 1970s. It was also one of the largest European exporters of guitars to the United States and the brand that first caught the eye of Mike Robinson, founder of Eastwood Guitars.

A significant part of the history of Pigini's company is also tied to that of the Lo Duca Brothers, American born businessmen who would later import Eko guitars into the United States. Eko produced organs and guitars for Vox and was a leader in the distribution of musical instruments in Italy.

Eko's business increased steadily through the '60s, with important bands in Italian pop music using them like The Nomads, The Rokes, and New Dada, among others. This helped Eko score the distribution deal with the LoDuca Brothers that would bring the electric guitars into U.S department stores. When coupled with a deal with Vox to share distribution rights Eko appeared to be the next big guitar company to break out of Europe. The glory was short-lived: with the deal between Eko and Vox ending in the early 1970s and with the LoDuca's shortly thereafter, Eko needed a new direction. The company buoyed itself through the ensuing decades thanks to acoustic guitar sales and has recently been able to return to their origins.

Current Eko Models

The Rock-VI is the reissue of the Eko original that is built with the look of a rocket ship. Its alder body is complimented by a maple neck, single coil and humbucking pickup choices with two way selector switch, BB tremolo, chrome die-cast machine heads and an industry odd 23 frets. This was the electric guitar popularized by the Italian band The Rokes in the early 1960s.

Another electric guitar displaying innovative (if not unusual) body style is the 700 Original. The body of the instrument is made from basswood with maple reprising its role for the neck and rosewood for its fingerboard. Eko's reissue incorporates two humbucking pickups, 3-way selector switch, and double-action truss rod.

Today Eko is still distributed nationally though its instruments are a rare find in the United States in vintage or reissued form. The company has also made a stout run at producing amplifiers and has seen some success in that market. This is quite in line with other guitar companies that have lasted through the birth of rock 'n roll. Fender began this way as a small repair shop selling quality built amplifiers, and today the majority of larger companies maintain their own sound amplification wings.

Above: the Eko 700 Original Reissue

The Encore Series of guitars is actually produced by John Hornby Skewes & Co Ltd and was designed with the aid of British luthier Trev Wilkinson. The Encore Blaster Series as it was named features all the subtle hallmarks of Wilkinson's design technique such as tonewoods, hardware, pickups, comfort, balance, playability and tone set. These work to set the Encore guitars apart, giving them a credibility which will surprise even the most experienced player and inspire the first time player to play. Encore Blaster Series guitars feature specially created vintage-voiced pickups to produce astonishingly accurate and authentic tone. The pieces built will look surprisingly like famous body styles from other guitar companies and should be seen as such. It's a "look for less" project.

Hardware, too, is fundamental to tone and performance. The Encore Blaster Series features custom-designed hardware and vibrato bridges, which significantly enhance the superb tone and playability of these guitars. Models are made to appear as Fender's classic Stratocaster and Telecaster electric guitars as well as Gibson's SG and Les Paul. They are geared in price to be that "starter instrument" for the first time electric guitar player with many packages offering a small amplifier, guitar picks, and cable with the purchase.

The Guitar Distributor as Shoppe

In the mid 1960s, a desire for independence in business led to John Hornby Skewes forming a small musical instrument agency and wholesale business based out of his home address in Garforth, near Leeds, England. Previously a sales representative with Hohner (another guitar company profiled here), followed by a short engagement with British guitar company Fenton-Weill, John Skewes had learned enough about serving the music trade to make the most of his own opportunity in his own business venture. With the enlisted aid of his wife Madge, his new business steadily began to take off,

and soon his home address was no longer capable of holding the now-considerable output of musical merchandise which by this time included some self-branded lines, and so the first of various local storage premises were acquired by means of expansion. They were at the mercy of whatever was on hand and available and at one time locations included the town's old cinema and car park, plus the police station.

In late 1965 and now firmly established as a limited company, JHS joined the burgeoning British government-inspired export market drive by securing their first international customers, reinforced by a company presence at the following year's Frankfurt Music Fair, since which time the company has attended annually with an ever-stronger presence.

Big Business Innovation

JHS was one of the first companies to appreciate the manufacturing benefits of a truly international catalogue, and since those early steps abroad, imported merchandise has taken precedence in the JHS catalogue, with the Far East and the USA playing a prominent role in providing JHS with catalogue supply. While this has been the aim of many Korean and other Asian based manufacturers for years, JHS is one company that has been able to accomplish it virtually overnight.

Over the past 44 years, John Skewes has become established as a figurehead in the British musical instrument industry. He was elected president of the Association of Musical Instrument Industries in 1987 and again in 1988. John continues his work in this area with an active role in the (now) Musical Industries Association, forwarding his ideal of promoting healthy trading practices backed up by positive innovation. He also sits on the Board of Management of the Music Trades Benevolent Society.

Epiphone was once its own company, begun by the son of a Greek timber merchant in the early 1900s producing mainly mandolins and banjos. The company enjoyed great early success through smart business practices and quality instruments and competed outright with many larger guitar companies of the early 1920s and 1930s.

These days it serves as the "more affordable" arm of the guitar juggernaut, Gibson, who bought the company in 1957 for $20,000. It is somewhat ironic that the current owner of the company was once its greatest rival to the point that in the 1930s, Gibson designed instruments for the sole purpose of competing with rival Epiphone.

Since that time, and under the financial wing of Gibson, Epiphone has crafted a name for itself in the guitar making arena as a semi-detached entity from its parent company, producing reissues of existing Gibson models as well as creating lines of their own.

Much of Epiphone's modern credibility came in the form of a visit from rock 'n roll royalty in the 1960s when Paul McCartney, George Harrison, and John Lennon each purchased a Casino model double cutaway electric guitar. The Beatles' rubberstamp served to boost the production value of Epiphone's electric guitar lines, which had floundered in the face of its already strong acoustic guitar sales.

Above: Sir Paul McCartney, playing his Epiphone

Left: the Epiphone Studio
WC
Right: a closer look at the
Joe Pass VS

Epiphone Steps Up Their Electrics

The company that had been relegated to producing more affordable models of Gibson's classic designs has garnered some attention of their own in more recent history. Whether that is due to the shifting concept of what is affordable or more to their ingenuity is unclear, what is for certain is that the marketability of guitars made by Epiphone is rising.

The company's version of the Limited Les Paul Custom allows the frugal guitar player the opportunity to have the same look and sound of the Gibson original for half the price. With the same vaunted visual vibe of the original, this Epiphone Limited Edition Les Paul has all the amenities of the original: 5-ply top, back, and headstock binding; bound rosewood fretboard; split diamond mother-of-pearl headstock inlay; and 4-ply pickguard. The brilliant silverburst finish is set off by chrome hardware with dual humbuckers on an alder top with mahogany back and set neck.

Epiphone has also turned its attention to the vintage SG guitar design. Popularized by such players as Eric Clapton and Tony Iommi of Black Sabbath, the SG has the reputation of being Gibson's heavier end of the spectrum, the most distorted. The SG Prophecy Custom GX Electric Guitar from Epiphone is based on the original SG design. But this Prophecy GX has 2 Dirty Fingers humbucker pickups. Other lavish, Prophecy features on this guitar include a highly figured quilt maple top, pearl knobs, strap locks, graphite nut, Grover tuners, a bound ebony fingerboard, unique blade inlay, and a deep, rich black finish. The hard maple set neck and 24-fret ebony fingerboard provide a playground two full octaves in length.

The SG Prophecy guitar's Gibson pickups are extreme-output units designed for more of everything; much more clarity and volume than a traditional humbucker and an incredible, aggressive, wide response. The Gibson Dirty Fingers pickup comes with a 4-conductor lead and is wax-potted to eliminate unwanted microphonic feedback.

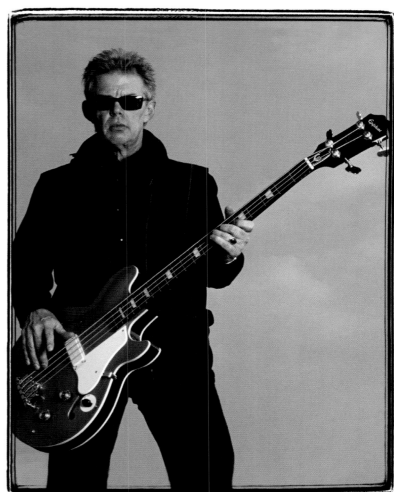

Above: Jack Casady with the
Epiphone Jack Casady Bass
Left: the Epiphone Wildkat
Opposite page: the Lucille model

In 1975, Hisatake Shibuya opened a shop called Electric Sound Products (ESP) in Tokyo. It provided custom replacement parts for guitars. In 1976, ESP gained a reputation as a provider of high-quality replacement parts, and during this time, ESP also began crafting guitars under the ESP and Navigator brand in the Japanese market.

ESP replacement parts were first introduced to the United States in 1983. ESP began crafting custom instruments for local New York artists in 1984-1985, where the company was based (a loft in downtown New York City on 19th Street; in 1989, the headquarters were moved to 48th Street), gaining popularity with speed metal guitar players like Page Hamilton (Helmet) and Vernon Reid (Living Color). It was around the same time that ESP began making necks for Kramer guitars, which only served to increase the range of companies under their roof. Many traits of the Kramer line are still visible, including neck construction and body bevels. ESP tooled up for Tom Anderson's shaved bolt on neck heel on the Schecter bodies, and has since become a feature of their house brand.

A Chance Meeting in Tokyo

In 1986, George Lynch discovered ESP while on tour in Tokyo. Lynch walked into an ESP shop looking for a replacement neck and learned that ESP also built custom guitars. As a result, his famous ESP Kamikaze was made. The company also released George Lynch's Kamikaze as its first signature model.

In 1993, ESP moved its headquarters again but this time it was relocated to Los Angeles. There, ESP opened an office on Sunset Boulevard in Hollywood. In 1996, LTD was created to produce ESP's high-quality products in a more affordable line of production. Soon after the introduction of the Korean and Indonesian-made LTD lines, ESP discontinued selling the majority of its Japanese-made flagship instruments in the United States due to the prices involved in exporting to the Americas. The lone exception was ESP's artist signature lines, which remained ESP (rather than LTD) models. In the early 2000s, ESP resumed shipping the standard Japanese-manufactured lines to the United States (where they are very popular among metal and hard rock players), albeit at greatly increased prices compared to the early '90s. Two key musicians to pick up an ESP guitar and ride it to notoriety and much-needed name-checks for the company were James Hetfield and Kirk Hammet of Metallica.

7-String and Baritone Electric Guitars

ESP has also built a reputation around electric guitars that lay outside the standard six-string model. The seven-string electric guitar rose to prominence in the late 1990s on the success of bands like Korn and Limp Bizkit. The baritone guitar was also used by Wes Borland (Limp Bizkit) and Mike Mushok of Staind. The seven-string guitar incorporates a low B string on top of the standard E whereas the baritone possesses a longer scale length so that it may be tuned lower than standard electric guitars. ESP currently produces several models of 7-string and baritone guitars under the ESP and LTD brand names such as the MHB-401 Baritone which weighs in at a 27inch length neck and the Viper-417 7-string with EMG active pickups.

Above and left: Metallica are great lovers of the ESP brand,and have heightened recognition around the world

California is the birthplace of Fender Guitars and the home of its namesake, Leo Fender, who began making custom guitars in a radio shop of his (then called Fender's Radio Service) in the 1940s. He sought to improve on the modified hollow body (acoustic) guitars jazz musicians were using to get their sound up over the timbre of trumpets and saxophones. Early electrified hollow-body guitars gave off a great deal of feedback when played at high volume; Leo thought he could improve on this.

In 1951, Fender introduced the Broadcaster, more of a prototype solid body electric that would lead to the design of the Telecaster, an electric guitar that has become synonymous with the Fender name. The Fender Stratocaster would follow the Telecaster in 1951 and cement the Fender as one of the most popular guitar makers of the modern era. Leo Fender did more than improve the electric guitar - he practically put it on the map. The company has had its ups and downs, from a sale to CBS, artistic limbo, and eventual to creative writing of the ship. Fender has weathered enough storms to show it's made of the right wood.

Left: Guitar God, Jimi Hendrix
Above: (left) Jaguar model, (middle)
Telecaster thinline and (right) Telecaster

The Fender Stratocaster

Often referred to as the Strat is a model of electric guitar designed by Leo Fender, George Fullerton and Freddie Tavares in 1954 and manufactured continuously to the present. It is a double-cutaway guitar, with an extended top horn for balance while standing. The Stratocaster has been used by many leading guitarists, and as such can be heard on many historic recordings. Along with the Gibson Les Paul, Gibson SG, and the Fender Telecaster, it is one of the most common and enduring models of electric guitar in the world. The design of the Stratocaster has transcended the field of music to rank among the classic industrial designs of all time; examples have been exhibited at major museums around the world.

In its original form, the Stratocaster was offered in a two-color sunburst finish, together with a solid deeply contoured ash body, a one-piece maple neck with 21 frets, black dot inlays and Kluson machine heads until 1957, when Fender started making bodies made from solid alder. There was also a set of available custom colors that was not standardized until 1960. These custom colors were mostly automobile lacquer colors made by Dupont and were available to the player for an extra 5% cost. The single-ply, 8-screw hole white pickguard was a unique concept that allowed all of the guitar's electronic components (except the recessed jack plate) to be mounted on one easy-to-remove surface. Subsequent Stratocaster designs (by both Fender and other imitating companies) have ostensibly improved upon the original in usability and sound, but vintage Fender models are still often worth large amounts of money and some prefer the timbre of older models.

The Stratocaster has been widely copied; as a result, the term "Strat," although a trademark of Fender Musical Instrument Corporation, is often used generically when referring to any guitar that has the same general features as the original, regardless of manufacturer.

Left: the famous Fender Stratocaster
Below: the Artist Series Jazzmasters
Opposite page: Keith Richards of the Rolling Stones and his Fender

Fernandes

Fernandes is a guitar and guitar accessory manufacturer that originated in Japan in 1969. They began as a company producing flamenco guitars chiefly and their brand of instruments bears their name to this day. As the company grew it expanded production to include more acoustic guitars, electric guitars, bass guitars, amplifiers, and accessories to become the biggest guitar manufacturer in Japan. During the 1970s, it became Japan's premier manufacturer of Fender copies; its Stratocaster copy, in particular, is generally considered by Fernandes to be a vastly superior instrument to the actual Fender Strats of the period. Though perhaps the actual creators of the Strat, Fender, would wholeheartedly disagree with such a statement. Fernandes also created a brand for Gibson replicas: Burny. A small wonder why American guitar companies brought so many lawsuits against Japanese guitar makers.

In 1992, following the history of success in Asia, Fernandes USA opened its doors in Los Angeles, California, and quickly established a presence in the American guitar market by offering quality instruments at affordable prices. By 1996, the Fernandes USA Custom Shop expanded its scope with further development in guitar craftsmanship. With models like the Ravelle and Nomad, and with the Sustainer System technology, Fernandes' Research and Development Department strived to find new ways to define the way the world plays guitar. Catering to everyone from the first-time buyer to the seasoned pro, Fernandes offers many options to meet their needs.

An invaluable understanding of the guitar player fuels their strong commitment to the consumer and the quality they demand. It is this approach that helped to establish Fernandes Guitars as the leading guitar manufacturer in Japan and to become a competitive manufacturer in the American market. Much like Japanese guitar maker ESP, Fernandes has garnered a good deal of attention from the global metal music movement and even country music that today has Fernandes touting a roster of talented musicians that support their products such as The Dixie Chicks, The Edge (U2), Phil Campbell (Motorhead), and Slayer. Fernandes continues to manufacture guitars that cover the range from inexpensive starter models to custom instruments of exceptional quality.

The Fernandes Vortex

The company's legendary V-shape that has been modified by countless other guitar companies throughout the years was recently brought back by "popular metal demand." Redesigned and revamped features alder body, finish-matching maple neck and set-thru construction with extended access to the high registers of the 24-fret Ebony fingerboard, Abalone binding diamond-shape inlays and FRT-11 locking tremolo system, with one and only EMG 81 active humbucker for full metal attack (metal guitar players are notoriously unfussy with knobs and selector switches), Fernandes Sustainer, die-cast tuners and ultra-comfortable body shape.

The Fernandes Vertigo

Another Fernandes trademark the famous Fernandes body style, the Vertigo has the distinction of becoming the first rebel in a family of traditional guitars. With the use of touring artist's suggestions, the company developed the Vertigo to be a familiar and versatile performing instrument. The Vertigo Elite features mahogany body and slim tapered set-neck, split trapezoid Abalone inlays in an ebony 22-jumbo-fret fingerboard, die cast tuners, FRT-11 Floyd Rose Licensed Locking tremolo, EMG 81 in bridge position, and Fernandes Sustainer in the neck.

Opposite page: (left) the unusually shaped Elephant Travel G model, (middle) the LE! , (right, the FR120S.

Framus

Framus originated in the town of Schönbach, which today is called Luby u Chebu in the area of Eger. The town itself has a long-standing history of musical instrument production with violins and other string instruments being manufactured and exported from Schönbach worldwide. There, in the Bohemian area of that famous town, the founder of Framus, Fred Wilfer, was born in 1917. When he heard about the expulsion plans of the allied forces that were going to affect his homeland in South Germany in WWII, he decided to build up a new business for his countrymen and the music industry in the West.

Even before the first train was going to transport violinmakers from Schönbach to other areas, Fred Wilfer contacted different government authorities in Bavaria and told them about his plans. The Bavarian government (as poor as they were) welcomed his ideas and asked him to create the ideal conditions that would increase immigration to Bavaria. For this reason he founded the "Franconian music production Fred Wilfer investment trust" (of which Framus is an acronym) in Erlangen on January 1, 1946. This factory became the central aim of the Schönbach violinmakers. When the first train transporting violinmakers from Schönbach arrived in Erlangen, he was the man in charge to find housing for them. He also made arrangements for the establishment of the first workshops.

The End of an Era

In an interview Fred Wilfer summarized his all-embracing concept with the following words: "It's not only important to produce instruments over a long period. It is important to produce customers." This motto is found in other Framus projects, as well. Eventually the price dumping by companies from Japan along with other factors, both external and internal, forced Framus into bankruptcy at the end of the 1970s.

Many aspects of the history of Framus are still in the dark. This is due to the bankruptcy of the company when almost the whole archives were lost. The Framus brand was revived in 1995 as part of Warwick GmbH & Co Music Equipment KG in Markneukirchen, Germany.

Framus Reboots

The past Summer NAMM Show saw a greater presence for Framus than it has had previously. "All day, the already packed Warwick and Framus Booth was filled with dealers and fans," writes Framus from their website. "As always, the Gear is being played all day long, and most leave with a sense of, 'I need one'…" The company that began with violins has made a serious push in the electric guitar market creating archtop models as well as newer style electrics to compete with the world's biggest guitar companies.

One such example is the Strat inspired Peter Fischer Signature. Proprietary electronics are featured throughout the instrument from Framus machine heads, tuners, to their in-house Plek Technology which creates a precise measuring technique which scans the neck on 132 measuring points (22 frets), every possible playing position on a guitar. The measurement is done with an exactly calculated pressure that simulates string tension, and the necessary neck relief is taken into account during this procedure. The dressing process does not take place as usual where all frets are leveled in one go; with the Plek procedure every necessary fret correction is sanded individually according to the measurements. The fret's crown is preserved even after the dressing process. The result is a completely level fret plane.

Right: a custom guitar made by Framus luthiers

G&L is a guitar design and production company founded by Leo Fender, George Fullerton, and Dale Hyatt in the late 1970s. Fender sold his company named Fender in 1965 to CBS, which freed him up to pursue other creative projects. He first tried designing and producing instruments for Music Man in the 1970s through his company CLF Research. When relations with Music Man soured, G&L was created to continue operations outside of Music Man. The G&L name comes from the initials of George (Fullerton) and Leo (Fender).

G&L instruments are similar to the classic Fenders, but with some modern innovations. They are built at the same facility on Fender Avenue in Fullerton, California that produced the early Music Man instruments. G&L instruments are not widely distributed but are highly regarded by many musicians and collectors. The relatively small scale of production further allows for more custom options than are possible on larger production lines.

After the death of Leo Fender in 1991, Fender's wife, Phyllis Fender, passed the management of G&L to John C. McLaren of BBE Sound. George Fullerton remained a permanent consultant until his death on July 4, 2009, and Leo's wife Phyllis remains as Honorary Chairman of G&L. George died of heart failure only weeks after his wife passed away. In a print advertisement for G&L, Leo Fender claimed the G&L line of instruments were "the best instruments I have ever made."

Innovations of George and Leo

The following are innovations in guitar design created and developed by George Fullteron and Leo Fender during the time they were creating instruments as part of G&L Guitars. These two men are great pioneers of the electric guitar and many companies today owe immeasurable debts to them for their ingenuity and creativity.

The Magnetic Field Design (MFD) pickups use a ceramic bar magnet in combination with iron pole pieces with adjustable height instead of the traditional Alnico magnet, and allows a player to set the pickup output per string, as opposed to the entire pickup as a whole in traditional single-coil pickup designs.

The Dual-Fulcrum Vibrato has two pivot points. The design aims to improve tuning stability, and according to some has a sound that is more mellow than a traditional bridge and it allows the player to bend notes up as well as down. See also Tremolo arm.

The G&L Saddle-Lock bridge utilizes a small Allan screw on the side of the bridge, to reduce side-to-side movement of the individual string saddles. The design aims to prevent loss of sustain due to this sideways motion by locking the saddles together.

The Tilt Neck Mechanism designed and patented by George Fullerton. This feature is no longer used, and was a carryover from Music Man production.

The Bi-Cut Neck Design involved cutting the neck lengthwise perpendicular to where the fretboard is later installed, routing a channel for the truss rod, then gluing the two neck pieces back together. As G&L moved production to CNC machines, this method was phased out as newer developments happened.

Opposite page: a closer look at the semi-hollow ASAT bass

Gibson

The Gibson Guitar Corporation, of Nashville, Tennessee, USA, is a manufacturer of acoustic and electric guitars. Gibson also owns and makes guitars under such brands as Epiphone, Kramer, Valley Arts, Tobias, Steinberger, and Kalamazoo. In addition to guitars, the company makes pianos through its Baldwin unit, Slingerland drums, as well as many accessory items. Company founder Orville Gibson made mandolins in Kalamazoo, Michigan, in the late 1890s. He invented archtop guitars by using the same type of carved, arched tops found on violins. By the 1930s, the company was also making flattop acoustic guitars, as well as the first commercially available hollow-body electric guitars, which were used and popularized by Charlie Christian. In the early 1950s, Gibson introduced its first solid-body electric guitar and its most popular guitar to date, the Les Paul. After being bought by the Norlin corporation in the late 1960s, Gibson's quality and fortunes took a steep decline until early 1986, when the company was rescued by its present owners (Fender has a similar story). Gibson Guitar is a privately held corporation (company stock is not publicly traded on a stock exchange), owned by chief executive officer Henry Juszkiewicz and president David H.Berryman.

Ted McCarty and The Les Paul Electric

In 1948, Gibson hired music industry veteran Ted McCarty. He was promoted to company president in 1950. During his tenure (1950–1966), Gibson greatly expanded and diversified its line of instruments. The first notable addition was the "Les Paul" guitar. McCarty was well aware of the strong sales of the Fender Telecaster. In 1950, Gibson decided to make a solid-body guitar of its own according to its own design philosophy despite the fact many other guitar manufacturers were contemptuous toward the concept of a solid-body guitar. Although guitarist Les Paul was one of the pioneers of solid-body electric guitar technology, the guitar that became known as the "Les Paul" was developed with very little input from its namesake. After the guitar was designed, Les Paul was asked to sign a contract to endorse the guitar to be named after him. At that point he asked that the tailpiece be changed, and that was his only contribution. The "Les Paul" was released in 1952, the tailpiece was changed in 1954. The "Les Paul" was offered in several models, including the Custom, the Standard, the Special and the Junior.

Left: the Gibson Les Paul '59 Reissue
Right: Jeff Beck playing his Les Paul

The Endless Lawsuits and Forgeries

It's difficult being on top. On multiple occasions, Gibson has sought legal action against other guitar manufacturers who implement similar body styles in their designs. The first such action was against Ibanez, which had fabricated near-identical copies of the Les Paul. This 1977 lawsuit was not over Ibanez's copy of the Les Paul's body shape, but instead for their use of Gibson's "open book" headstock shape (even though Ibanez had redesigned their headstock to be a near-identical copy of a Guild headstock in 1976).

More recently, Gibson sued Paul Reed Smith Guitars, forcing them to stop making their Singlecut model, which is much less similar to the Les Paul in appearance. The lawsuit against PRS was unsuccessful: in 2005, the United States Court of Appeals for the Sixth Circuit reversed the lower court decision and ordered the dismissal of Gibson's suit against PRS. The decision also immediately vacated the injunction prohibiting the sale and production of PRS's Singlecut Guitar. Paul Reed Smith Guitars announced that it would immediately resume production of this guitar model, which has since proved highly successful.

Guild is another brand that made copies of Gibsons. Aside from the above-mentioned companies, there have been countless others producing unofficial Les Paul copies, including among others Tokai, Stellar and newcomer Myaxe, a company based in Changle, China. Manufacturers of the Les Paul clones refuse to call their guitars copies such as in the case of Myaxe, which says theirs were an innovation of the solid bodies. Myaxe do not say what these innovations were/are. Whatever the case, Gibson's place in the pantheon of American guitar companies is a permanent one, and its imitators are the greatest testament to that fact.

Right: the Gibson SG - this model was originally an adaptation of the Les Paul, but he did not like the shape so his name was removed from the guitar and it was renamed the SG
Opposite page: the Motley Crue

Godin guitars are manufactured at one of six factories in Canada and in the United States.

"Why not just have one giant guitar factory?" writes Godin. "Although there are some obvious inconveniences associated with spreading ourselves out this much, the upside is that these smaller operations promote a more intimate working environment which gets everybody more involved and this is reflected in the instruments themselves." Godin guitars are assembled at the company's Richmond, Quebec, Berlin, and New Hampshire factories. The necks and bodies are all built at their original location in La Patrie, Quebec.

What is significant about Godin's construction methods is their desire to keep their workshops on shore. It allows for greater oversight in the production process and more adherences to the original intent of the guitar's designer, usually founder Robert Godin. From the company's beginning they have divided these factories between their acoustic and electric guitars lines and say that the company began their electric factories as part suppliers (mostly necks) for other guitar companies. "You might be amazed to find out how many different guitar brands are all being produced in the same handful of factories," writes Godin Guitars. "We're not telling you this because we want to divulge somebody's secrets but simply to let you know where we're coming from." This time spent producing guitar parts for other companies allowed Godin to see the dimensions future competitors were working with and used that knowledge to build their own innovations into the designs of what are now their current run of acoustic and electric guitars.

Godin believes the guitar is a fashion statement. They do not back away from this ethos for one moment, constructing instruments that are at once eye-catching and structurally sound. Indeed Godin has continued to delve for greater breadth in their conceptual mind of guitar creation, building unique instruments such as the Glissentar, an 11-string, fretless, acoustic/electric guitar. With such innovations rolling out it is exciting to see what Robert Godin and his team will do next.

Godin Electric Guitars

The Radiator, from Godin's Performance Series, is priced to suggest an entry-level instrument for the electric guitar player.

It features a short scale but is constructed of the same quality tone woods that other Godin models are: chambered silver leaf maple (body), rosewood (fingerboard), and rock maple (neck). Godin style, low-noise pickups provide the Radiator with cutting distortion with each pickup being wired with its own volume control that makes for a wide range of tones at the player's disposal.

The LG SP90 is a variation of Godin's classic LG design which now incorporates figured flame maple tops and cream binding. The LG SP90 Flame combines a 24" scale, mahogany neck and a solid mahogany string through body design to deliver accomplished tone and ease in playability. Two single coil Seymour Duncan pickups rest beneath its strings giving this Godin electric the tone of early blues electric guitars created by Fender. That kind of comparison is a passing matter for Godin who has truly forged their own path creating guitars both acoustic and electric that are unique, appealing and instantly playable.

Above: John McLaughlin performs with the 4th dimension
Right: a closer look at the Godin Radiator

Greg Bennett

Greg Bennett Guitars are produced by the Samick Music Corporation. After 40 years of producing guitars, the Korean musical instruments manufacturer hired industry veteran Bennett to give their guitar line a complete overhaul, with the goal of improving appearance, sound quality, and build quality.

Bennett started redesigning the instruments at his studio in Nashville, Tennessee, after which the search for the electronics and woods took place. The new Samick guitars, now under the name of Greg Bennett Guitars (still an 'S' in their headstock however), possess a wide array of professional level parts including pickups designed by Seymour Duncan, machine heads from Grover and bridges by Wilkinson. The new woods used in the production are also high quality; the search for distinctive tonewoods ranged worldwide, netting woods such as ovangkol and ebony from Africa, rosewood from India and rock maple from North America. These woods are increasingly rare and show Samick's attention to detail in looking outside the box to maximize musical potential. Greg Bennett Guitars also manufactures a range of stringed instruments including electric, acoustic and archtop guitars, electric and acoustic basses, and mandolins, banjos, ukuleles and Autoharps.

Poetic names were given to every line of instruments to stimulate better product identification and also to give a more "high-end" feel. Perhaps the most common distinctive feature in all these new instruments (apart from the mandolins, banjos and autoharps) are the signature angled-back headstock. These headstocks feature the new logo right at the top and are designed small intentionally, as Greg states that bigger headstocks rob more energy from a vibrating string, causing less sustain and thereby reducing overall sound potential. Poor design in this area leads to a flat sounding instrument.

Who Is This Seymour Duncan?

Seymour Duncan is a company that has produced some of the most ubiquitous guitar pickups in music today and currently has a line of effects pedals. The company was founded in late 1978 by guitarist and luthier Seymour W. Duncan in Santa Barbara, California.

The first artist signature pickup was the SH-12 "Screamin' Demon" model, created for George Lynch (Dokken, Lynch Mob). Seymour Duncan also wound the humbucker in Eddie Van Halen's Frankenstrat guitar. Another well-known Seymour Duncan artist is the late "Dimebag" Darrell Abbott, with whom they collaborated on a signature pickup, the SH-13 "Dimebucker", which has been used on Abbott's tribute guitars, produced by Washburn Guitars and Dean Guitars (featured in this history). Nearly every major musician of the 20th and 21st century worth any amount of salt has collaborated with Seymour Duncan in designing a unique pickup for their signature instruments.

Bennett Guitars

The Bennett Ultramatic UM3 bears a double cutaway body style similar to that of electrics designed by Paul Reed Smith. Its thin silhouette body reduces the overall weight of the instrument giving it an easy playability and holds up well with the guitar's alder body and maple top. Duncan humbucking pickups are used as well as Grover tuners giving the guitar an appearance of the "high end model" that Samick had intended when Bennett was brought in to take over the project.

Gretsch

Friedrich Gretsch founded the company that bears his name in Brooklyn in 1883. By 1895 the founder of the burgeoning guitar workshop was dead, leaving the business to his son, Fred Gretsch. As a young man Fred took what his father had created and built it into the popular guitar company that would see it take over a 10-story building on Broadway twenty years later. Acoustic guitars were the best sellers for Gretsch in their early days before the advent of electronics and as Fred left his company to Fred Jr. in 1942 the Gretsch "sound" was stronger than everyone. Three Freds down, one to go. While Fred Jr. served his country in the Navy, his brother Bill managed the company. Rock 'n roll went quite well for the Gretsch family and in 1967 music industry giant Baldwin purchased the company.

Gretsch remained the property of Baldwin for almost 20 years until 1985, when a determined Fred W. Gretsch bought back his great-grandfather's company to put it once again in family hands. That makes four Freds. The production center for Gretsch Guitars has since moved to Georgia, where it continues guitar as well as drum production to this day.

Left: a closer look at the G5120 Electromatic Hollow Body Limited Edition Above: (left) the Bo Diddley, (right) the Country Club model

The NAMM Show

The acronym NAMM originally stood for the National Association of Music Merchants, but has evolved from a national entity representing the interests of music product retailers to an international association including both commercial, retail members and affiliates. The long form of the name is no longer used as it no longer truly represents the intent of the organization, and it is simply known as NAMM, the International Music Products Association. The group has worked to create initiatives for music in inner cities and with urban youth, the creation of scholarship and grant funding in a continuing effort to help create new music lovers and producers of all ages.

The Artists That Make Gretsch

As a company, Gretsch owes much of its beginnings to the legendary Chet Atkins and its current success to big band revivalist Brian Setzer. Gretsch currently has four of its electric guitar models devoted to the Setzer line, one of which is the Black Phoenix. The new G6136SLBP Brian Setzer Black Phoenix was designed and built to Brian's detail-oriented, meticulous specifications. Features include 1959 Trestle bracing, TV Jones Classic pickups, pinned Adjusto-matic bridge, Bigsby B6C vibrato tailpiece, and silver sparkle binding. Schaller straplocks and Grover Imperial machine heads are standard equipment. The model is finished in gloss black nitrocellulose lacquer.

A newcomer to Gretsch is Fall Out Boy lead singer/guitarist Patrick Stump, whose own signature model was recently released by the guitar company. The G5135PS "Stump-O-Matic" rides a set-in neck on 3 MegaTron pickups with electronics designed by Tom "TV" Jones to allow for pickup selections that would satisfy the artist's stage needs. If it seems that guitar companies tend to fall over themselves in their courting of major rock acts to front their products, it's because they do. The benefit in a musician playing an instrument built by a specific company is free PR for as long as that artist is getting on stage, performing, doing music videos, and brushing their teeth. Anything.

Grimes

Grimes Guitars is helmed by luthier Stephen Grimes and was started in 1972 when he set up his own guitar workshop in Seattle, Washington. As early as 1974 he began making acoustic archtop guitars, which then led to flat top guitars in the early 1980s. It was around this time that the luthier moved his shop from the left coast to the blue shores of Hawaii. Grimes has said the climate was more conducive to guitar production with lower humidity levels and consistency of temperature though it is difficult to believe such a move was not motivated in part by the fair weather and great surf found in the area.

Grimes Guitars is a relatively small shop producing instruments slowly and meticulously by hand. Close attention to detail, such as tuning top and back plates, often missing in production guitars, is fundamental in each instrument. The advantage to building a few instruments at a time from start to finish is being able to control the response and tonal characteristics as each instrument progresses. This process takes time, and a commitment to achieving the fullest tonality and brilliance the wood has to offer. About 20 guitars are produced in the shop annually. While not exclusively an electric guitar shop, Grimes has an important place in the guitar making industry for its dedication to the core values that started many of its biggest companies.

Grimes Bird of Paradise

The Bird Of Paradise model is a semi-solid body electric guitar that features carved curly maple top and back plates with a Honduras mahogany core. The body is 60% solid, providing excellent sustain without the unnecessary weight of a solid body and without the feedback problems inherent in many acoustic/electrics. The balance of the guitar is excellent, and at approximately 7.5 pounds, it is comfortable to hold for longer periods of time. The Bird is also available with an oval soundhole. Pickups and electronics are designed to the individual guitar player's specifications, as each instrument produced by the Grimes shop is a custom creation.

Small Workshop Innovations

In 1991, Stephen Grimes teamed up with musical innovator Ned Steinberger, a luthier in his own right who famously created electric guitar and bass models without headstocks, to produce an experimental flat top guitar in which the soundboard is not put under tension, as it is in standard flat top, classical, or arch top guitars. Using a unique bridge system, the "stress free" guitar directs the string tension to a tailpiece, allowing much lighter braces to be used without fear of an exploding or imploding soundboard. This system makes it possible for the top to vibrate more freely, producing a loud, full, open tone. This is in stark contrast to the tradition of the X-bracing system which was developed as the be-all end-all in acoustic/electric guitar manufacturing. It has been nearly 20 years since Grimes and Steinberger developed this method in construction and we have seen other companies slowly catch one with similar experiments in design such as Godin.

Right: the Grimes Montreaux in an unusual blue finish

Emile Grimshaw, born October 1880 in Accrington, Lancashire, was a banjo player in the early 1900s. He played in his own quartet, the highly respected Savoy band. He made quite a substantial amount of recordings and was well known for his music and tuition books. Emile Grimshaw Jr., his son, was also a very skilled player and musician who played with the Jack Hylton orchestra, and also contributed to compositions which were credited only to Emile Grimshaw. To add to the confusion there was also Monty Grimshaw (Emile the elder's brother) who was also an accomplished musician.

The early guitars were constructed in a similar fashion to the banjo, in that the guitar had a separate detachable back (on later models the back was fixed, due to bad vibration from the back which was only held by two thumb screws). The main body of the guitar had a large circular hole in the back, this it was perceived would amplify the sound. It's a matter of open debate if this form of construction worked or not, but they are very interesting and unique sounding guitars.

Models Produced by Grimshaw

This range of guitars were branded Revelation, they also made a range of standard format guitars under the Hartford brand. Both types were available as archtop "F" hole, or flat top roundhole models. Both the Revelation and Hartford models were available in three levels of trim and both were available as "Hawaiian" models. In the 1935 catalog Grimshaw listed the Premiervox electric guitar, which could be plugged into a radio or special amplifier. This interesting guitar was assembled in England from parts imported from Rickenbacker, but with many components manufactured in UK.

Like many early companies in the early 1900s, Grimshaw didn't make it long out of the 1960s. During the 1950s they crafted several ranges of archtop guitar models as well as jazz style electrics and were encouraged by the sales of their Les Paul copy, and it was their best selling model in the 1960s. Four hundred models of that guitar were produced though that was the height of their business. They also "borrowed" style elements from the Gretsch Guitar Company. Grimshaw continued to limp along until the 1980s, when Emile Junior died and all activity from the company stopped.

The Ramifications of Big Business

Electric guitar history is a field unto itself. Companies have risen and fallen in the face of wars, music crazes and hostile takeovers since the 1900s, this only serves to show the vast untapped potential that may have come had these workshops survived. In some cases larger guitar manufacturers have been able to rescue struggling companies and assist them. Gibson and Fender have been buying up guitar workshops in similar fashion since they were rescued from the grips of an apathetic corporate master by dedicated employees and guitar businessmen. Sadly, that ship sailed for Grimshaw, but there is hope that their archtop and other electric creations may yet resurface.

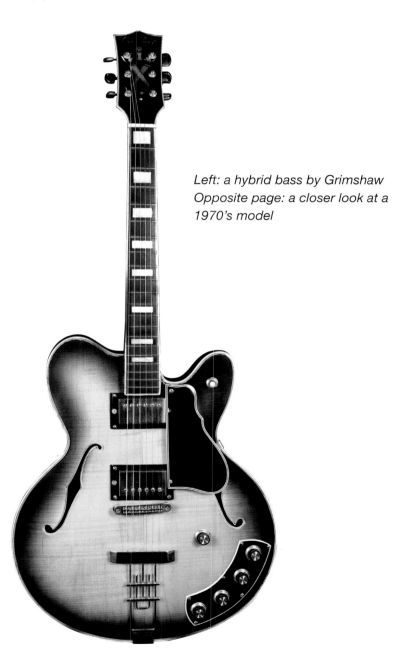

Left: a hybrid bass by Grimshaw
Opposite page: a closer look at a 1970's model

The Swedish based guitar company began building instruments in 1958. The first Hagstrom Deluxe solid body guitars featured a distinctive sparkle and pearloid celluloid finish, an ingenious repurposing of materials previously used in their accordion production line. Over the years, Hagstrom expanded their line-up to include hollow body guitars like the Viking and the Jimmy, electric basses including the legendary 8 string, and Hagstrom's flagship models, the Swede and the Super Swede. Hagstrom also produced a series of acoustic and classical guitars in the early '70s. When Hagstrom ceased production in 1983, the guitars became instant collectors' items, and the love and respect for these fine instruments continues to be celebrated by musicians around the world.

Hagstrom guitars boast the original glorious Hagstrom sound and distinctive style, and they are built to the same stringent quality standards. All materials and hardware are sourced from the world's finest suppliers, and technological advancements including their patented H-Expander Truss Rod and exclusive Resinator Fretboard guarantee that these are the finest guitars on the market. Dweezil Zappa, son of the famed Frank Zappa, swears by Hagstrom guitars and plays them on the "Zappa Plays Zappa" tour. As Dweezil prepares songs for the set, he also spends a considerable amount of time tweaking his gear to get the vintage tones used on the original recordings, and that is exactly where the Hagstrom Viking comes into play. "The Viking feels amazing and it has a great natural sustain," states Dweezil talking directly to Hagstrom. "It has an awesome vintage tone right out of the case, so then I can use my outboard gear to sculpt the sound as necessary."

Left: a P46 Sweetone guitar in blue.
Opposite page: Franz Ferdinand performing live onstage, playing 1959 Hagstrom P46 Sweetone guitar

What Is a Truss Rod?

A truss rod is a guitar part used to stabilize and adjust the lengthwise forward curvature (also called relief) of the neck. Usually it is a steel rod that runs inside the neck and has a bolt that can be used to adjust its tension. Thaddeus McHugh, an employee of the Gibson Guitar Company, applied for the first truss rod patent in 1921, although the idea of "truss rod" can be encountered in patents as early as 1908.

When the truss rod is loosened, it allows the neck to bend slightly in response to the tension of the strings. Similarly, when tightened, the truss rod straightens the neck by resisting the tension of the strings. It is desirable for a guitar neck to have a slight relief in order that reasonably low action is achieved in the high fretboard positions, while at the same time, the strings ring clearly in the low positions. Improved action in the higher positions also allows for more accurate intonation, which can be achieved with less compensation at the bridge.

Truss rods are required for instruments with steel strings, which operate at high tensions. Without a truss rod, the guitar's wooden neck would gradually warp beyond repair due to applied high tension. Such devices are not normally needed on instruments with lower tension strings, such as the classical guitar, which uses nylon strings. Truss rods also allow the instrument neck to be made from less rigid materials, such as cheaper grades of wood or man-made composites, which without the truss rod would not be able to properly handle the string tension. The neck can also be made thinner, which improves playability. In fact, the possibility of selecting cheaper materials is pointed out in the 1923 patent as an advantage of the truss rod. Prior to the introduction of truss rods, the neck would have been made of a very rigid wood, and relief was achieved by planing the fingerboard: more expensive material, and more demanding construction technique. The truss rod is, in effect, an innovation born out of necessity, but one that has allowed larger corporations to flourish by using cheaper woods and lighter materials.

Hamer

Hamer Guitars is an American manufacturer of high quality guitars. It was founded by guitar designer Jol Dantzig in the Chicago area with his business partner Paul Hamer in 1973, and early instruments featured guitar designs created by Dantzig. Originating in the Chicago area, Hamer Guitars is generally seen as the first "boutique" electric guitar brand that specifically catered to pro musicians. Kaman Music Corporation acquired the company in 1988. Hamer offers a range of electric guitars and electric basses and since its foundation concentrated on producing high-end instruments with vintage aesthetics as well as creative innovations.

How It All Began...

Hamer began publicizing their instruments with small ads in guitar magazines in 1974. By 1977, the company employed up to seven workers. Most of the work up to this point had been one-off custom variations on the original "Standard" and "Flying V" guitars. During this period Hamer's customers were limited to big-name touring groups such as Bad Company, Wishbone Ash, Jethro Tull and Savoy Brown. In order to appeal to a broader market, the first "production" Hamer called the "Sunburst" debuted in 1977. Production was reportedly set at around 10 guitars per week. During this time the company steadily gained more popularity with the high profile patronage of Cheap Trick guitarist Rick Nielsen and the use of Hamer 8 and 12 string basses in their music.

1980 brought a move to larger quarters in Arlington Heights, which is a suburb of Chicago. The staff had grown to 12, and Hamer Guitars continued to launch new models such as the Special, Cruisebass, Prototype, Blitz and Phantom. Hamer left the company in 1987 in order to pursue a career in retail, leaving the company without a sales manager. Kaman Music was approached for sales and distribution as a result. Seizing the opportunity to expand into the high-end electric market, Kaman offered to purchase Hamer in 1988. During the 1990s, a process of diversification at Hamer expanded the product offering into lower and lower price points which allowed other companies such as Paul Reed Smith Guitars to reap the benefits of Hamer's exit from the high end of the market. This reportedly precipitated Dantzig's departure from the company in 1992.

Current Hamer Models

Hamer has expanded its popular XT Series with a new Sunburst Quilt top model for 2009. The new Sunburst Quilt 2 (SATQE2) features an ivoroid bound mahogany body, capped with a striking arched, quilted maple top. The mahogany set neck is adorned with a rosewood fingerboard and MOP crown inlays. Powered by two EMG-H4 humbucking pickups, the Hamer XT Sunburst Quilt 2 is ready to overdrive your amp into sweet sustain. Available in Dark Cherry Burst and Transparent Black finishes.

Below: the Slammer Daytona model.
Opposite page: Glenn Tiptop of Judas Priest

Harmony

Harmony was at one time the production king of American instruments, and during its peak accounted for over half the guitars built in the United States each year. In 1892, Wilhelm J. F. Schultz purchased a two-room loft on the top floor of the Edison Building at Washington and Market Streets, later the site of Chicago's Civic Opera House. The company's first business was the sale of two guitars in 1892 to the Chicago Music Company. Schultz's business grew quickly and housed 40 employees by 1894. In 1904, Schultz and crew settled into their own three-story, 30,000 square foot plant with a new wing added in 1906. By 1915, Harmony had a quarter of a million dollars in annual sales and 125 employees.

Jay Kraus was appointed vice-president and in 1926 succeeded founder Wilhelm Schultz as Harmony's president, and along with Fred Gretsch Jr., Hank Kuhrmeyer of Kay, and others, he ultimately became one of the great captains of the Chicago guitar manufacturing community of the 1930s-1950s. Jay Kraus was one of the six men who met in 1947 to found the American Music Conference (AMC) and served as president of both that organization and NAMMM, forerunner of NAMM, or National Association of Music Merchants which runs a very important vendor convention every summer.

Mergers and Acquisitions

In May 1939 Harmony bought several brand names from the bankrupt Oscar Schmidt Company including La Scala, Stella and Sovereign; the latter two were used on many of Harmony's most popular guitars. During this period Harmony substantially increased its trade names to include Valencia, Monterey, Harmony Deluxe, Johnny Marvin, Vogue, and many more. We have seen this business strategy moving forward with other U.S. guitar companies and it is becoming the model with which they maintain success.

In 1941, Harmony reportedly manufactured about 130,000 of the 250,000 American guitars produced each year. The music industry retail sales grew steadily through 1957, and Harmony was a primary benefactor of this growth.

Big Business Strikes Again

From 1961 to 1969 Harmony continued to grow, expanding to a plant of 132,000 square feet of manufacturing and warehouse space with around 600 employees. Then as imported instruments began taking a larger share of the American market, the company was purchased by a conglomerate along with some other companies. There was heavy indebtedness, and the factory equipment and other assets were sold at auction to satisfy the creditors and they finally liquidated.

Today, President Charlie Subecz owns Harmony Guitars. In 2008, Charlie decided the time was right to bring back the old Harmony style guitars by launching a series of vintage reissues. Fourteen models from the 1950s and '60s were selected, including the Rocket, Bobkat, Meteor and more along with a signature Ritchie Valens classic.

Ritchie Valens Signature Stratophone

The body of this signature Harmony model is made from nyato (similar to teak) with maple for its neck, and rosewood at the fingerboard. Kluson tuners and a Harmony Hershey Bar pickup give the Valens its unique tone and resonance. The downside? It only comes in green.

Left: Mark Ribot
Right: Rolling Stones' Brian Jones

Former employees of the Gibson guitar factory founded Heritage Guitars in 1985. In the early 1980s Gibson was faced with excess production capacity (and there are those that claim, a difficult relationship with its labor union), closed its historic Parsons Street factory in Kalamazoo, Michigan and relocated much of its production to its factory in Nashville, Tennessee. Some of the Gibson employees who did not want to move their homes and families to Tennessee started production of guitars under a new name, "Heritage." The company set up their new factory in part of Gibson's former Kalamazoo premises, but produced instruments in much smaller numbers than Gibson had, but unsurprisingly was forced to produce instruments in smaller numbers than Gibson had.

The Heritage line initially consisted of electric and acoustic guitars, electric basses, mandolins, and a banjo, which was consistent with what the luthiers built for Gibson. The line was eventually narrowed to electric guitars only. Although most Heritage guitars were, and continue to be, based on Gibson designs, a few of their early electric guitars were based on modified Stratocaster and Telecaster designs.

Methods of Production

Apart from the use of a Plek automated fret-dressing machine to grind the frets to the correct crown and intonation, Heritage guitars are largely handmade, without the use of CNC machines for woodworking. Heritage, however, is clear about the fact that their guitars are indeed manufactured, with no claims that they are handmade.

During the first several years of the company, Heritage advertised its guitars in the usual guitar magazines. These advertisements made it clear that Heritage was making guitars on Parsons Street in Kalamazoo without ever mentioning Gibson by name, and the company began to develop an image as the alternative to Gibson at a time when Gibson was going through a period of transition and rebuilding. By the 1990s, perhaps in an attempt to keep costs low or because orders were numerous enough, the company all but stopped advertising. This lack of an advertising presence significantly limited and even diminished the brand's name recognition among guitarists. Recent years have seen a growth in the Heritage name, in part due to word of mouth on Internet forums devoted to guitars and guitar gear, including the Heritage Owners Club, which debuted in 2007.

Homage Over Outright Theft

In general, Heritage makes guitars that are similar to Gibson's products, but which the company's advocates and fans would say are constructed in a much more "handmade" manner and with much greater individual attention to the instrument by the builders. Part of this increased attention to detail is a result of Heritage being a smaller operation than Gibson, and some of it is likely a reaction against the cost-cutting practices that developed at Gibson during the Norlin years (practices that Gibson would later work to remedy as well).

The design of the Heritage H-150 solid-body guitar is clearly modeled on the Les Paul Standard, while the H-575 resembles the ES-175 and the H-535 reinterprets the ES-335. There are differences between most of the Heritage models and their Gibson counterparts, however, which is artful skirting of the rules on Heritage's part (Gibson is a bit lawsuit happy). For example, all Heritage full-body semi-acoustics have solid wood tops, while many of the Gibson guitars of this type had laminated tops after World War II. Both the 575 and the 535 are thinner than their Gibson cousins. Heritage has also introduced several new designs, most notably the Millennium models, which employ a "semi-solid" body that is more solid than a traditional semi-hollow design, but chambered, and thus less solid than a typical solid body.

Above: Joe Lewis Walker
performs on his Heritage

Highland

Canadian based Power Group Ltd. premiered their new line of guitars, which would be called the Highland Guitar Company at 2008's NAMM Show. Their aim was to produce finely crafted instruments that would be viewed as both pieces of art and able-bodied guitars. Highland focused on attractive and ergonomic designs that would appeal to all levels of skill creating solid-body, archtops, and semi-acoustic models.

Power Group is an award-winning North American distributor and sales agent of select musical instruments, professional audio components and consumer electronics. Since 1989 they have worked on building a dealer network to help them (the music dealers) build their sales volume and product offering. Power Group's dealer network spans North America and overseas. They service their dealers from their Canadian and U.S. warehouse partners to ensure the most efficient and cost effective means of supporting musical instrument dealers and their customers. To the dealer, Power Group brings the market's best products with a focus on quality, technical advantage, profit potential and groundbreaking design. The company backs this with competitive pricing, inventory, supply chain management and prompt technical support.

Albion HEG-700

Made from chambered mahogany and a quilted maple top, the Albion by Highland carries the little black dress quality in its appeal: quite understated in its beauty but nevertheless a classic. Two PAF type humbucking Alnico-V pickups with chrome plating give the Albion velvet resonance and sustain through its Indian rosewood fingerboard and mahogany neck. Flair amenities include ebony control knobs with position markers and a laser engraved wooden truss-rod cover.

Cool Fire HEG-1200

Tribal ornament acrylic adorns the Cool Fire electric guitar from Highland. Its body is similar to the Albion in that it is built from chambered mahogany and an arched maple top. Grover black machine heads adorn the Cool Fire with 2 uncovered Alnico-V humbuckers giving it the chugging sound that is implied by its sleek yet aggressive looks.

Bop Cat HEJ-600

Laminated spruce carries the warm toned appeal of this archtop Highland model. Maple is used for the guitar's back with Alnico humbuckers, gold plate covered, continuing their starring role as suppliers of Highland's tone and pop. An archtop trapeze tail piece provides a classic touch to the instrument and exemplifies the guitar manufacturer's aim to create aesthetically appealing guitars that are affordable for the everyday musician. Highland likes to call their instruments "acoustic art" which is a high aim considering the weighty company that pervades the art guitar market with Godin, Luna, and others producing beautifully crafted instruments that, while perhaps not having Highland's price tag, have every ounce of come-hither potential.

Left: the HEG-1200SBR
Right: the HEG-600FB and
HEJ-600

Hodson

Hodson guitars is owned and operated by Darren Hodson. Of his company, he writes, "We are a guitar company owned and run by guitarists, for guitarists. Here at Hodson Guitars, our goal was very straightforward: to build 'real' guitars of a giggable quality for an unbelievable price."

"Having spent years in the industry," Hodson continues, "playing, buying and selling guitars of all shapes and sizes, makes and prices, we have been working very closely with one of the best manufacturing facilities in the modern world to bring you this stunning collection of guitars. Each and every one of our guitars was designed and conceived with the working musician in mind, for the players who need a reliable, quality instrument that will stand up to the punishment of 4 to 5 gigs a week, pounding the venues around the circuits."

The Jackhammer Series

A dead ringer for a Fender Stratocaster, the Jackhammer series is one of the most affordable lines from Hodson, which is based in the United Kingdom. The body is built of solid alder (same as the Strat), bolt-on construction with die-cast chrome machine heads, and a rosewood fingerboard. Its three high output single coil pickups lay in the same positions as the iconic Stratocaster. The custom version of the Jackhammer bears less resemblance to the Fender designed electric with its ash topped body and Hodson headstock.

The LP Series

As the name would suggest the series for Hodson is modeled gingerly after the Les Paul series of electrics created by Gibson. The "black beastie" was created as an attractive, UK based alternative to the pricier models created by American based guitar companies, and as an affordable one weighing at no less than half the cost. Tone knobs are placed in a similar fashion as the Les Paul, as are the dueling gold covered humbucking pickups. The '59 Model recreates that original Les Paul feel right down to the sunburst finish.

Why No Litigation?

The difference between Hodson's designs and those of Japanese guitar manufacturers, which Gibson battled in court for many years, is something relatively simple. Hodson isn't posing their product as something it is not. That is to say, Hodson is quite open with the homage aspects of their instruments whereas Japanese guitar makers were somewhat shy about admitting the facsimile to the consumer. This allows the creations of both guitar companies to stand on their own merits, to allow Hodson to create affordable instruments for a British guitar player that may not be able to afford an American import, and for Gibson to continue its long tradition of quality and innovation.

Hofner

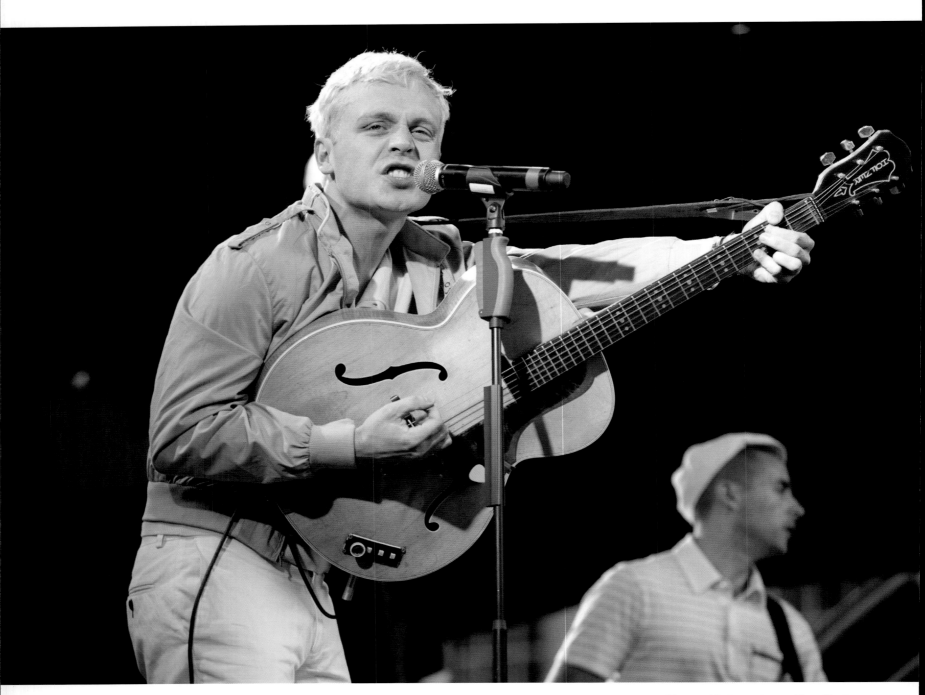

Above: Hofner player, Ben Hudson performs in Somerset
Right: Chris Rea

Karl Höfner GmbH & Co. KG is a German manufacturer of musical instruments, with one division that manufactures guitars and basses and another that manufactures string instruments. The company was made famous by The Beatles' bassist Paul McCartney's use of their left-handed 1962 Höfner 500/1 model as well as John Squire's well-publicized use of a custom Jackson Pollock paint-job semi-acoustic guitar while in The Stone Roses. Today it is known as the "Beatle Bass" or "Cavern Bass" after the Liverpool club where The Beatles played in their early days, and the first bass player of The Beatles, Stuart Sutcliffe, used a 500/5.

The Höfner Company was founded by luthier Karl Höfner in the city of Schönbach in Germany in 1887 and soon became the largest manufacturer of string instruments in the country. His sons Josef and Walter joined the company around 1920 and began spreading the brand's reputation worldwide. The company suffered some upheavals during and after World War II, but survived and continued to thrive. The company built new factories in Bubenreuth in 1950. The iconic instrument McCartney rode to fame is a tribute to the area that the company was created in, as it has been known as an area of violin craftsmanship for many years.

Where Hofner is Today

In 1994, Höfner became part of the Boosey & Hawkes Group, and was able to expand and upgrade its facilities with the influx of cash. In 1997, the company moved from Bubenreuth to Hagenau. After a near-bankruptcy in 2003, Boosey & Hawkes sold its musical instrument division (including the Höfner and Buffet Crampon companies) to The Music Group, a company formed by rescue buyout specialists Rutland Fund Management, for £33.2 million. Höfner remained a part of this conglomerate until January 2005, when The Music Group sold the company to Klaus Schöller, who has been the General Manager of Höfner for many years. In mid-2005, The Music Group (having lost many of its component manufacturers) stopped distributing Höfner in the USA, and Chicago firm Classic Musical Instruments (CMI) picked up the distribution.

The company maintains a small roster of archtop, jazz style and acoustic guitars but is a shade of its former glory. None can be considered completely electric guitars as the majority rely on the hollow body of the instrument to sustain sound though some do utilize pickups. Hofner did create electric guitars and most will fetch a decent sum on the collectors' market, the last of which was created in the 1980s.

Current models are electric jazz style guitars from their "Verythin" line that include a signature instrument for guitarist John Stowell. The instrument is a bright spot for Hofner, which is celebrated for its flexibility and broad tonal palette. Hofner's versions of the semi-hollow body can portray the subdued warmth of a full hollow body, or the bright and primary hues of a solid body. The solid tonewood block inside the body is carefully crafted to fit exactly the curved top and back of the guitar. This construction provides a sensitive response and excellent sustain. Every "Verythin" employs a hand-fitted solid spruce sustain block that does not use tone bars. These features reduce the potential for feedback, accentuate the tonal punch and preserve the guitar's acoustic qualities.

Hohner

Founded in 1857, Hohner is both the oldest and largest harmonica producer in the world. Thirty years after their founding, Hohner was producing more than 85,000 harmonicas a year. The years have seen the once exclusively produced instrument give rise to other products, including recorders, accordions, percussion and, more recently, guitars. The rise of rock 'n roll would force Hohner to add guitars to their more traditional harmonica and accordion production in the face of shrinking sales and revenue bloodletting. At first, however, they were not the quickest to adapt to the popularity and universal appeal of the guitar.

By the 1960s, it was clear that Hohner as a company had missed the boat on the acoustic/electric guitar movement worldwide. Ernest Hohner, then current CEO of the family owned company, did not provide Hohner with enough lateral movement and bounce to create eye-catching and musically relevant instruments. He believed rock 'n roll to be a fad, the guitar the flag bearer for a movement that would flash out of its pan. Thankfully for Hohner, his retirement in 1965 marked the path for new direction.

The ensuing decades would see Hohner to finally pursue guitar production in greater earnest as well as move some of their harmonica production to the United States. Forming Hohner/HSS with Sonor and Sabian, the United States division of Hohner began to distribute guitars and cymbals. Hohner also began to produce guitars under its own brand. Revenues for Hohner still continued to shrink despite these changes, reaching a tipping point by 1986. Hohner was forced to make layoffs, and Kunz-Holding GmbH & Co. obtained a controlling interest in Hohner around this time.

The Harmonica is Not King

Hohner in large part is still an accordion and harmonica based company with only a small portion of their development projects going to guitar building. "The Black Prince" is one such electric guitar project that sports a Fender Telecaster body style. The body is made from alder with a traditional "C" shaped neck and rosewood fretboard. The guitar incorporates three hand-wound Haussel pickups in a S/S/H pattern, which means the single coils are placed first with the humbucking pickup placed closest to the heel of the guitar. A Wilkinson/ Gotoh Tremolo system adds weight to the guitar's playability as well as in a literal sense. Many that have bought or simply played the Black Prince have commented on the overall heft of the instrument.

The Ergonomic Guitar System or EGS is another in the small lineup of Hohner electric guitar creations. The futuristic Alder Body features the patent-pending "Ergo-Wing," which allows body height adjustment for perfect playing position while seated, making it perfect for practicing. The EMG pickups and Shadow Piezo-equipped tremolo system make the EGS an incredibly versatile instrument. The guitar also features Schaller locking tuners, allowing the guitar to compensate for lack of body (the guitar body is artfully designed but small) breadth. These two models show very divergent styles for Hohner and give a small glimpse that going forward, there is still the drive to invent and follow new ideas.

Left: 1953 poster advert for Hohner Harmonicas
Opposite page: Paul McCartney with his Hohner bass circa 1965

Ibanez

It began in 1908 with Hoshino, a company selling sheet music out of a storefront in Nagoya, Japan. The Ibanez brand name dates back to 1929 when Hoshino Gakki (founder of the company that bore his name) began importing Salvador Ibanez guitars from Spain. When the Salvador Ibáñez workshop was destroyed during the Spanish Civil War in the early part of the 1900s, Ibanez guitars were obviously no longer available, so Hoshino Gakki bought the "Ibanez Salvador" brand name, rights, and started making Spanish-styled acoustic guitars in 1935, at first using the "Ibanez Salvador" brand name, and then later using the "Ibanez" brand name.

In the company's infancy, Hoshino copied existing European guitar body designs. This continued into the '50s and '60s when Hoshino (now distributing under the Ibanez name) began exporting guitars to the United States, which featured interesting body designs in an attempt to find a niche in the guitar world. Some actually made it to department stores and were sold to the public. When this attempt to catch the American eye failed, Ibanez turned a decade later into copying existing body designs. Ibanez labeled copies of Gibson, Fender, and Rickenbacker guitar designs soon began to appear in stores.

The Receiving End of Gibson's Ire

The period immediately following the 1960s is sometimes referred to as the "Ibanez lawsuit period." Needless to say, American guitar companies were not pleased with Ibanez producing guitars which copied their seminal body styles and signature acoustic/electric models. The lawsuit that followed put a stop to Ibanez as well as other lesser known guitar companies that were producing body styles synonymous (and copyrighted) with more famous guitar companies.

By the mid-'80s, with the interest in instrumental rock guitar on the rise, Ibanez collaborated with players such as Steve Vai, Joe Satriani and Paul Gilbert and brought out the JEM, JS, RG and S models. Today, present day versions such as these models are still considered the standard in hard rock and instrumental rock guitars. Ibanez has rightly made a name for itself in that niche of guitar production that is crafting instruments with the professional player or virtuoso in mind.

Modern Marveled Models

A heavier mahogany battleaxe than the S, the SZR is thicker for more screaming, fat tone. Its 25.1" neck has a different feel than the 25.5" scale of the S. The SZR's contours make up for any weight difference with a physical comfort that's ideal for any guitar player utilizing more energetic play and general thrash. The set-in neck sits under a vine inlay, which traipses onto the SZR's two NeoZ-B humbuckers that provide the guitar's powerful, saturated sound without muddy intonations.

Steve Vai is one of the few guitarists universally acknowledged as one who has changed the way musicians think about what a guitar can really do. His signature Ibanez guitars are no different. The JEM7EAFX is a Vai model that houses DiMarzio Breed pickups (two humbucking, one single coil) in its basswood body. The JEM Prestige neck is comprised of maple and walnut.

Jackson is a guitar manufacturer originally owned and operated by Grover Jackson, a partner of Wayne Charvel of Charvel Guitar Repair. It started with the creation of the "Rhoads" V model guitar, originally designed and used by guitarist Randy Rhoads, which was then used and promoted by Vinnie Vincent of KISS, after the death of Rhoads. As discussed earlier, Jackson put his name on the Rhoads rather than the Charvel name because he felt the design was too shocking for Charvel's more conservative clientele. This model inspired Grover to start the Jackson Guitar Company.

Wayne Charvel sold his interest in the Charvel name to Grover Jackson on November 10, 1978. The shop was located in Glendora, California, and manufactured guitars in this location from 1979 to 1986, when the company merged with IMC (International Music Corporation), a Texas based importer of musical instruments. The factory then moved to Ontario, California.

Fender Steps in

In 2002, Fender Musical Instrument Corporation purchased Jackson/Charvel, and operations were moved to the Fender factory in Corona, CA. Fender is now manufacturing guitars that are almost exactly like (thanks to their purchase of the rights) the original San Dimas Charvels. Both Jackson and Charvel models are being produced at Corona. This had short-term negative consequences, as much of the artists who were on the company's roster list in the 1980s and 1990s left to endorse other guitar companies. Though significantly improved since the buyout, FMIC's own creative direction for the company is still stated to be a problem with Jackson. Most, however, see that some of the new things that FMIC has instituted, such as the fairly low prices on high end USA models and improved quality in lower end models will help the company experience a turnaround shortly. Signs of this are already cropping up with new artists signed to signature series deals and new instruments being developed virtually all the time.

Elements of a Jackson Guitar

Jackson Guitars has become known for its slender and elegant models, often with an aggressive look popular with harder rock and metal music. Almost all Jackson (and many Charvel) guitars share the typical Gibson Explorer-like pointy drooped headstocks. Various guitar models feature a reversed pointed headstock with the tip directed upwards. Another hallmark are the company's "shark fin" fret inlays, which inspired other successful guitar companies such as Ibanez to develop a similar design to that of Jackson's original, called "shark tooth".

The Signature Series from Jackson shows the company's tremendous versatility in creating electric guitars that are both artful and powerful. The KE2 Kelly, which is featured in their upcoming release Jackson: Bloodline, (a book that details the best Jackson guitar designs over their history) combines angular body design carved in alder with copper snakeskin paint job and a pair of Seymour Duncan humbucking pickups to provide the heavy tone that is suggested by the guitar's wickedly carved shape. Artists that currently play Jackson guitars compromise a rogue's gallery of metal musicians from Mack Morton (Lamb of God), Matt Tuck (Bullet for My Valentine), to Slipknot.

Jay Turser

Jay Turser is a guitar manufacturer owned by American Music & Sound. Jay Turser makes acoustic, electric, bass, and jazz guitars as well as amplifiers. This company is known for its affordable guitars and has received several awards as testament to that fact. In 2004 Turser received Guitar Player Magazine's Readers' Choice Award for Ultimate Value for their JT-200 line. It makes a variety of models including Flying Vs, double-necks, hollow body archtops, homages to the Les Paul and many others. One unique model is the Surf Master, which resembles a Fender Jaguar but has 3 P90 pickups.

American Music & Sound

Located in Agoura Hills, California, American Music & Sound is the exclusive distributor of the world's finest pro audio, DJ, and MI products. American Music & Sound (AM&S) distributes Allen & Heath professional audio mixing products, Focusrite Audio Engineering signal processing, Hagstrom Guitars, KV2 Audio speaker systems, EtherSound products by NetCIRA, a division of Fostex Japan, Nord Keyboards, Novation Digital Music Systems synthesizers and controller keyboards, Turbosound professional loudspeaker systems, Vestax DJ and club sound equipment, Quik Lok performance structures, Jay Turser Guitars, and Walden Guitars.

The JT-50 Series

The JT series bares the body style of the Gibson SG to a T. They even have a double 6/12 string version in their JT series, the same body design Gibson used when creating its 12/6 made famous by such guitarists as Jimmy Page and Claudio Sanchez (Coheed and Cambria). Even the pearloid fretboard inlays smack suspiciously of Gibson's design.

JT-200 Series

Turser's design sports a sharper cutaway than the original groundbreaker but the layout of the body design is quite similar to the Les Paul. Possible exceptions occur with the Serpent JT-200, which incorporates a serpent pearl in its rosewood fretboard. The JT-200 Pro looks like the seldom seen Gibson Double Cut right down to the toggle switches and pickup selectors.

The Modern Series

Truser begins to shine when they leave behind the trodden earth of already fleshed out body designs. Their Modern Series highlights designs such as The Warlord, which displays a modified V body style and scorpion-esque headstock. The JT-Shark looks like, well, a shark. Each is individually hand painted in "mako shark color" and uses two single coil and one humbucking pickup.

Turser rounds out their collection with more retreads of Fender Telecaster models and even Dobro style acoustic guitars. The appeal of these body styles is understandable but the stagnancy it perpetuates within the music industry as what is an "acceptable or viable" instrument is a hole not easily dug out from. For progress to be made in the electric guitar, progress similar to what Leo Fender and George Fullerton accomplished years ago, there must be a concerted effort to reshape the canon of what is popular. Turser is showing signs of life, better late than never.

Johnson

Johnson Guitars USA was founded with the goal of competing in the open market against guitar giants like Gibson and Fender. Their wide swath of electric guitars is pushing the envelope on body style and electronics while garnering ever-increasing amounts of attention from players and fans. Their Exotic Series alone displays some of the most unusual and creatively intense body styles in more recent history which all served to make quite the splash when they premiered at 2008's NAMM Show.

The J23 Standard

A melting look to the heel of this electric guitar sets off the tropical American mahogany body construction. Several options are available for the guitar player to choose between such as the abalone or pearl inlays, gold or chrome hardware, tune-o-matic or vibrato bridge system. Even the neck of the guitar is customizable at 22 or 24 frets. All J23 electric guitars are handmade in the United States

The Assault Guitar Series

Three Johnson USA models are available crafted in the shape of jets (The Russian MIG, German Tornado, and F15 Eagle). Each are crafted to the individual guitar player's or collector's specifications and portray the given war plane distinctively down to its wings. Playability may perhaps be an issue thanks to the guitar's increased body width but the look is no less inspiring. As if that weren't enough, the other "wing" of the series includes three assault rifles with varying accessories. They are the M60 Assault Guitar, AK87/91, and the Tommy Gun AKA Chicago Typewriter. All models are designed with the intent of being fully playable, not just showpieces, and Johnson has done their best to make good on that promise. Built of solid mahogany (similar to the J23) each model works in dual humbucking pickups and whammy bars with adjustable bridge and tailpiece for added comfort in playability.

Exotic Series by Johnson

For the collector or musician that values the electric guitar as art before function, the Exotic Series is perfect. Johnson presents the models in three distinct areas: Shark Attack, Egyptian and Dragon Series. Shark Attack has two body styles, Great White and Hammerhead. The Egyptian Series shows three Egyptian gods: Anubis, Horus, Osiris, Apophis, and Bast. Lastly the Dragon Series has three models:

Aztec Dragon, Chinese Dragon—Dragon King, and Japanese Dragon—Water Dragon.

Appropriately, the Egyptian electrics are constructed of African mahogany, gold plated tuners at a 14:1 gear ratio, with each model coming equipped with a removable death mask (face underneath). All are handpainted, signed and dated by the artist/luthier. The Dragon models have unique features such as the 9-string configuration on the Water Dragon, scalloped back fit of the Dragon King, and six in-line tuners of the Aztec Dragon.

What is so refreshing about Johnson Guitars USA is the attempt to push the envelope, to expand what is acceptable and marketable in the world of electric guitars, a world that has been all too dominated by just several popular body styles over the last 50 years.

Above and left: two unique examples from the Johson range

John Birch

John Birch Guitars began in Birmingham UK in the early 70's with its founding members John Birch, John Diggins and Arthur Baker. They introduced a new way of guitar building with redesigned body construction giving better playability, a new range of pickups and some advanced switching options, which competed alongside other guitars and guitar companies of that time.

These quickly found favor with bands of that period and many went on to become world famous in later years. In 1993, John Birch and John Carling restarted the business from Nottingham, UK, and again came up with a new more advanced range of pickups and used modern paint processes to improve the finish still further. In 2000, John Birch died and left the business to John Carling to carry on and this is the current business that we see offering a range of products and services today.

A Famous Customer

Tony Iommi of Black Sabbath came to Birch's shop after having his ideas rejected by the major guitar manufacturers of the time, such as Gibson and Fender. Iommi was looking for someone to make him a guitar with a 24-fret fingerboard and high power/low noise pickups. Iommi's red Gibson SG Special received some modification in the form of a recovered Gibson P-90 in the bridge position and John Birch's own Superflux in the neck position. This guitar is in the Times Square Hard Rock Cafe. In 1975, Birch built Iommi his black 24-fret, cross inlay SG Special. This was the main guitar used on the albums "Technical Ecstasy," "Never Say Die," "Heaven and Hell," and "Mob Rules."

This guitar is currently housed in the Miami Hard Rock Cafe. John Diggins also built Iommi's Jaydee SG, which features a custom wound pickup by Diggins in the bridge position and a standard Biflux in the neck position. Business was clearly looking up for John Birch and friends.

The Jaydee SG also has peeled and cracked paint due to a rushed finish job. During a world tour, the guitar was left in a hot car on a date in Brazil, and the finish bubbled and cracked due to the heat. This guitar was first used for some overdubbing on "Heaven and Hell," but quickly became Iommi's main electric guitar.

Ahead of Time Developments

The list of Birch's famous clients included Roy Orbison, Brian May, and Dave Hill. While Birch created many electric guitars the strength of the company appeared to be their pickups of which there are about 20 variations. The majority of pickups utilize Alnico or ceramic magnets whereas Birch utilized oversized cobalt steel magnets and very fine copper wire, which allows for a more powerful sound. The result was a lower level of feedback, or hum, and a greater level of sound than was commonly available from other humbucking pickups of that time.

The Birch shop also built a guitar for Tony that featured the ability to remove and replace pickups. The pickups plugged through the back into slots which had quick connectors that allowed them to be pulled and replaced easily, and didn't require any soldering. This allowed for more tonal options than any standard guitar, no matter how complex its wiring. Geezer Butler also had some basses made by Birch, one of which can be seen in the music video for Black Sabbath's "A Hard Road."

Above: Roy Orbison pictured here with the Traveling Wilburys Bob Dylan and George Harrison
Opposite page: Tony Iommi with his main guitar the Jaydee SG

Jones

Jerry Jones, as a guitar company, is based out of the musically rich town of Nashville, Tennessee. The company specializes in making electric guitars and basses based on Danelectro's designs from the 1950s and 1960s. They also make some unusual instruments, like six string basses, baritone guitars, sitar guitars, the short octave 12-string and the guitarlin, which is a cross between a guitar and a mandolin.

Custom Retro Models

Many of the company's instrument designs borrow heavily from the early designs, and Jones does not shy away from this fact. JJ Original guitars have original body and headstock styling and many have distinctive matching neck and body paint. The coke bottle headstocks are fixed with their traditional "Jerry Jones Guitars" red triangle decal. The company has taken pains in using traditional shaped pickguards that includes the white "curlicue" pickguard used on Jones' Shorthorn "Jimmy Page" style guitar. Switching for 2PU models utilizes a heavy-duty bat-handle switch while the 3PU models use standard 5-way Strat switching. High quality Gotoh hardware, keys, and bridges are used throughout with all models fitted with Jerry Jones' very own homespun lipstick tube pickups. All guitars are handcrafted in Nashville, Tennessee, USA.

JJ Original Shorthorn Guitar

Another example of a classic 1950s instrument with modern refinements, the traditional double cutaway body shape gives great access to upper frets. The Shorthorn guitar has a traditional retro styling matched with JJ's Lipstick-tube pickups producing a real honking tone. Large radius fingerboard also makes the Shorthorn a great option for those guitar players wishing to incorporate slide technique into their play style.

Longhorn Guitarlin

Innovative body design indeed; the Guitarlin is a version of the longhorn bass built as an electric guitar complete with its deep double cutaways and sharp horns. It combines elements of both the mandolin and standard guitar for an octave range of nearly four steps. This instrument features a 25" scale length and a 21-fret neck, Indian rosewood fingerboard, Gotoh tuning keys, hum-canceling pickup wiring, JJ's in-house lipstick tube pickups, and Gotoh bridge with adjustable saddles.

Dolphin Nose Single Cut

A revisioning of the 1950s classic style guitars popularized by Danelectro, the Dolphin Nose Electric is hollow-bodied to increase tone resonance. Its unique pickup wiring is a Jones exclusive for the design and works as in other models to reduce hum without utilizing a double coil or humbucker. Its lipstick tube pickups account for the signature '50s style "honk" tone with Gotoh tuning keys allowing for increased stability of its strings.

The fact that Jerry Jones are available across the United States is evidence that this guitar model still has some appeal left, and that the market is not entirely consumed with reproducing Fender and Gibson electric guitar models. Though these guitars are themselves from an earlier era, their interest with modern players shows that their creators were capable of creating timeless classics. They aren't as inexpensive as the originals, however, with retreads posting prices of four figures.

Right: John Oates of Hail and Oates is a Jones devotee

The Kay Guitar Company primarily produced inexpensive department store style (similar to modern day DiPinto and Eastwood) guitars from the 1930s to the 1960s. Kay Guitars is a part of the Kay Musical Instrument Company that has manufactured professional and student instruments since the 1890s. Kay (along with several other companies) lays claim as the first company to start production of electric guitars in the United States in 1928.

In 1957, president Sydney Katz introduced the Gold "K" line of archtop and solid body electric guitars to attempt to compete with major manufacturers like Fender, Gibson, and Gretsch. The headstocks from 1957-1960 are highly valued among collectors and feature a reverse painted plastic overlay similar to the Kelvinator logo. The guitars also included art deco patterns on their tops. It was difficult to get players to take Kay's high-end entry seriously in the face of already established lines by other companies, and the Gold line was discontinued in 1962. The company was sold to Valco in 1967 and driven out of business two years later by low cost Asian import guitars.

The Current Kay Production Line

Kay's current line includes low priced acoustic, electric and bass guitars, and moderately priced banjos, ukuleles, mandolins and resonators. They also sell the Chicago Blues line of inexpensive harmonicas. The electrics are mostly retreads of the more successful body designs of other guitar manufacturers and they are, indeed, low priced.

Their models emulate the Gibson SG, Les Paul, and Casino with Fender's lone body style choice being the Stratocaster. The ramifications of Gibson's loss to Paul Reed Smith in a recent lawsuit have apparently opened the doors for all guitar companies and it is apparent that none have wasted time in capitalizing on that turn of events.

Kay recently produced a reissued model of its Jazz II electric guitar. It features "Kleenex box" pickups to provide its smoky, thickly populated club tone that Kay describes as the "classic '50s sound." The K161 Electric Guitar was originally created in 1952. This guitar used hand-wound pickups and a separate center chamber that allowed for greater resonance and distortion without feedback.

Value in Vintage Reissues

Appeal in vintage guitars is garnered through scarcity. It's a matter of economics, plain and simple. That is, if a guitar is no longer available and there is demand for that particular instrument, then there is value in a prospective guitar company unearthing its design and giving it another go in the workshop. Luthiers are often able to update the production methods and use cheaper materials to lower the cost of what would otherwise be an instant collectible that allows current players to have a window through time into what an instrument sounded like 30-40 years ago. This leads to a similar unearthing of musical styles such as the recent rebirth of the fuzz-based guitar sounds of the '60s with bands like Silversun Pickups (latest album "Swoon") and White Stripes who are often compared to UK based Band of Skulls.

Left: the popular KB24B
Opposite page: a closer look
at the K161VBK

Kendrick

Kendrick Amplifiers and Guitars is a Texas-based company that was started by Gerald Weber in 1989 near Austin. They were the first to build a reissue, vintage vacuum tube type amplifier, which was called the 2410. Their 2410 amp was a recreation of the legendary Fender 5F6A Tweed Bassman. They were also the first to introduce a reissue, vintage-style speaker in 1989. 1994 saw Kendrick begin building and selling guitars. Their luthier, Tony Nobles, is world-renowned, and has built a guitar for the Smithsonian "Guitars of Texas" exhibit.

In 1998, Kendrick's president, Gerald Weber, began conducting "Tube Guitar Amplifier Seminars" to teach others how to service and modify their tube amplifiers. He has written several books on this topic and produced a DVD, "Tube Guitar Amplifier Servicing and Overhaul," in 2002. All Kendrick products are manufactured, one at a time, by hand, in their factory in Kempner, Texas. The Kendrick Team ensures that every aspect of each amp passes the company's stringent quality standards.

The Kendrick Canary Guitar

This model was developed while doing research on another project. Kendrick was attempting to find the perfect tonewood for a speaker cabinet, but instead they discovered an obscure tonewood from Brazil. Perhaps the most impressive characteristic of the Brazilian canary wood was its sonic focus and purity. The wood possesses a clarity not found in other woods.

Besides being louder than other woods, the wood didn't break tones down into subtones as other more often used woods tend to, thus allowing a more round, bass flute-like quality to the sustaining portion of the note. Kendrick as a company decided to try the Brazilian wood as a top for an electric guitar. They created a version of their Townhouse guitar with the canary wood cap instead of the traditional maple.

The result is quite impressive, now called the Canary Guitar. It sounds acoustically better than other guitars and is so loud without an amplifier that is could compete favorably with an acoustic guitar. All the other features are of finest quality and are in keeping with their other guitars. The body is old growth Honduran mahogany and everything is finished with hand-mixed nitro-cellulose lacquer. All guitars are hand-built by their master luthier from the handcarved neck to the carved top. This guitar compares favorably with other guitars selling for two to four times the price.

The Kendrick Continental

This model takes obvious inspiration from the Fender Stratocaster but instead of being built as a cheaper version, Kendrick has attempted a higher end model. The Continental is Kendrick's take on how a bolt-on-neck electric guitar should be made. The offset body is made from a one-piece plank of lightweight alder hardwood and is contoured for balance and comfort. The neck is the company's standard offset, rounded "V" shape, designed for an uncommonly "natural" grip. The neck is made of maple with a rosewood fret board. The Continental is an encouraging break from the norm from Kendrick and one that not many companies have undertaken. Instead of making the traditional and most popular body styles cheaper and more ubiquitous, they have sought to push the form to see how elegant it can be.

Klein

Steve Klein has been creating genre-bending instruments for many years with his models being placed in the hands of many of music's finest players such as Steve Miller, Joni Mitchell, Andy Summers, Joe Walsh, Bill Frisell, Lou Reed, and David Torn. Michael Hedges played a Klein electric harp guitar, and Stanley Clark, Billy Sheehan and Sting along with others play Klein designed basses. Klein's skill as a luthier is beyond question, and he hails from a family with a long history of excellence in instrument craftsmanship. Klein's grandfather was an ornamental caster in Austria. He took his family out of Europe to escape the war, settling first in St. Louis and finally in northern California. Steve has inherited his grandfather's talent of transforming natural elements into practical and beautiful works of art.

In 1991, Steve Klein and Bob Taylor began designing the AB series acoustic bass, which is now in production in southern California. Klein has also constructed a 19 string electric harp for musician Bob Gore and worked with other artists to develop ergonomic, headless electric guitar models. Klein had done well as a company until it was sold to Lorenzo Guzman. Production all but halted, some orders for custom instruments going unfilled. In 2006, the company announced they would no longer be accepting orders, and then in 2007, Klein's guitar website went down apparently for good. Steve Klein remained silent.

A Breaking Story

According to Rob Irizarry of eLutherie.org, who broke the story in 2008, Steve Klein was planning a comeback. "I have recently been talking with Steve Klein," Irizarry wrote. "Steve and I were talking about working together. I was going to be making the Klein bodies with my CNC machine but the distance between us was too much of a hassle factor with the cost of shipping wood back and forth, et cetera, and he has found a more local approach. What does this mean? All I should really say, because I do not want to talk for Steve, is that Steve is 100% definitely actively planning on starting up again, most likely within six to nine months from now. His new shop is being organized right now. I should not say much more than that but he is alive and well, a great guy, and is set on jumping in again."

Klein indeed returned, setting up shop in Vineburg, a small town in California, and wrote a book detailing his life and works.

Below: the strangely shaped Klein GK
Opposite page: Lou Reed playing the GK

Kona's mission statement announces them as "guitars made for players by players," yet does not go on to name one luthier that works for their company, and what exactly they play. The electric guitars that are featured by the company are mainly based on oft-emulated popular body styles. Some would claim that this is a big box corporation, masquerading as a small lutherie.

The Big Box Music Store

The neighborhood guitar shop has been under attack in recent years in North America by larger corporate entities selling high volumes of instruments and wider arrays of products: the Wal-Mart of the musician's world. Epiphone, Gibson, and other companies have been able to take advantage of higher capacity factories in other countries to allow for cheaper production costs that in turn are turned over to the guitar player purchasing the instrument. The result (in theory) is a higher percentage of sales and profit because the instrument is more affordable and therefore more appealing.

The Internet is also the playground of the warehouse style music, which will ship an inventory of literally thousands of guitars (acoustic and electric), basses, drums, even recording equipment anywhere in the world and for (usually) a discounted price and free shipping. That's hard to compete with. Guitar companies now have many outlets to sell their instruments and one with low production costs such as Epiphone may use that affordability to ride out any economic storm.

The problem with many of these (Internet purchased) instruments, and a problem that differs from the handcrafted guitars of companies like Johnson USA and Breedlove, is that many of them require a degree of fine tuning once they have been purchased and are delivered to a musician's doorstep. "If someone comes in with a guitar bought online from one of those websites, I won't work on it," says one guitar technician at a local guitar shop in the central portions of Pennsylvania. "That's their fault."

Opposite page:
Left, the K35FMN
Middle, KEL5TSB
Right, KEL5BK
This page: KESSTSB

Kona Guitar Models

Their Double Cutaway Solidbody Electrics bear the Stratocaster shape though with different headstocks. The three different models are set up as different variations of the Fender classic with the first model being outfitted with three single coil pickups, the second with a heel humbucker and the third repeating the second in every electronic means.

The company's electric guitars then move through a small series of Gibson knock-offs from the Casino model, the Jumbo Archtop, and of course the Les Paul.

Kramer

Kramer Guitars is an American manufacturer of electric guitars and basses. Kramer produced aluminum-necked electric guitars and basses in the 1970s and wooden-necked guitars catering to hard rock musicians in the 1980s. Kramer is currently a division of Gibson Guitar Corporation and was one of the most popular guitar brands of the 1980s. According to sales records, the guitar company was the bestselling brand of 1985-1986. At the height of its popularity, Kramer was considered a prestige instrument and was endorsed by many famous musicians.

The company was founded in the late 1970s by Dennis Berardi and Gary Kramer, an associate of Travis Bean, to manufacture aluminum-necked guitars. Gary Kramer, Dennis Berardi, Peter LaPlaca (a vice-president at Norlin, parent company of Gibson), and investor Henry Vaccaro joined forces to open a plant in Neptune, New Jersey. Soon thereafter, Gary Kramer moved to Los Angeles and his connection with the company would be in name only.

Gone the Way of So Many Others

The original Kramer Company came to an end in 1990, due largely to financial difficulties. The company lost a lawsuit with Floyd D. Rose (tremolo maker) over royalties, and an infamous "firesale" of surplus necks, bodies and hardware was held out of New Jersey.

By 1995, Henry Vaccaro owned the Kramer brand, and incidentally was the only one of the original partners interested in continuing in the guitar business. He tried one last time to produce Kramer guitars from surplus parts, in the Neptune plant, but only a few hundred were made. Henry Vaccaro started making aluminum-necked guitars under the name Vaccaro Guitars, but that did not last long.

Gibson to the Rescue

The Kramer brand was sold out of bankruptcy to Gibson Guitar Corporation. Gibson's Epiphone division has produced guitars and basses under the Kramer brand since the late 1990s, mostly factory-direct through Internet based commerce. The numbers were encouraging and it appeared Kramer was experiencing a resurgence of interest in their brand. Epiphone has been reissuing classic Kramer models, including the "1984 Model" (a tribute to Eddie Van Halen's famous "5150" guitar used from 1984-1991), the "Jersey Star," (a homage to the Richie Sambora signature 1980s Kramer) and most recently, the "1985 Baretta Reissue (a standard slant-pickup Baretta)". Gibson assembles these high-end instruments in the USA using American components.

In 2007, a Kramer Striker controller was created for Guitar Hero III for the PS2 under a licensing agreement with Gibson Guitar Corporation. A Kramer Focus was also available as an in-game guitar, as was one of the earlier aluminum neck model Kramers. The Kramer Fatboy has been featured in Guitar Hero III: Legends of Rock and Guitar Hero Aerosmith. It has been a long road back for Kramer who are still searching for those newer musicians to carry the banner of the brand like Eddie Van Halen and Richie Sambora did for the company in the 1980s. With a strong company like Gibson backing them, it's clear that Kramer won't be going away anytime soon.

Above: White Snake performing live

OVERDRIVE — CLEAN —

OVERDRIVE

GAIN   LEVEL   LEVEL   LC

Lakland Musical Instruments was an idea that took a little longer to germinate than normal. Long before that first bass made its way to the NAMM show in July 1994, it would be early in 1992, and Dan Lakin had begun to buy used basses, vintage basses that caught his eye. As he would buy one, another would pop up and spark his interest. Before long, he had to sell some to buy others. This was done via word of mouth or by placing ads in newspapers. The young "company" found that the bass world is generally a small world. Once they opened the door, that's all it took for word to spread.

The Road Ahead for Lakland

Some of these basses would need minor adjustments or restorations, which led Lakin to a local luthier named Hugh McFarland. Hugh was an experienced craftsman and quite accomplished at fretwork. When Hugh re-fretted a bass, Dan felt it played better than it ever had. "As the number of basses Dan bought and consequently had to sell continued to grow," writes Hugh McFarland for Lakland, "Dan and I began to publish our own sell list. At first, whenever we could get newsletters out, we got them out. As basses stockpiled in our basement and we saw a used bass business evolve out of Dan's interest, we were printing and mailing thousands of newsletters a month. At first, I folded them by hand in our basement, stapled them with my stapler from college, and banded them for mailing. As the numbers grew, we bought an old paper-folding machine to expedite the process. I started coming to work with Dan, setting up in a caged dungeon-like room down in the bowels of the Lakin family's factory, the paper-folding machine and me. Dan was still working upstairs for the family business. The used basses were Dan's and my thing on the side."

Into the Modern Era

1995 would mark the first concert with a Lakland bass. A local Chicago producer, Jim Tulio, set the tiny Lakland team up with Rick Danko, bass player for The Band. It was arranged that Jim, Hugh, and Dan would take the bass to the hotel to meet Rick. If he liked the bass, Lakland was in. In 1995, Danko was not the bass player he was when he took the stage for "The Last Waltz." He was much heavier than in 1976. Although Rick was very friendly and nice and they were enamored with him, he could hardly stay awake or alert during their visit. While today his substance abuse problems are common knowledge, it was news to the boys of Lakland at that time. At one point, he offered to order them room service, and while he was on the phone, he actually did fall asleep. Rick liked the bass and agreed to play it the next night. The night Dan Lakin met him was the night before the band's show opening for The Grateful Dead at Soldier Field, which turned out to be Jerry Garcia's final show with The Dead. Lakland's star would rise, even as Garcia's burned out.

Larrivee

Jean Larrivée first became interested in the guitar as a teenager. At 20, with no other musical training to speak of, he made the decision to take up a serious study of classic guitar. Four years into this study, he was introduced to German classical guitar builder Edgar Mönch, who was working in Toronto at the time. Jean expressed interest in learning how to build classical guitars, and Mönch invited him to visit his shop, and so began an apprenticeship.

Jean built his first two guitars under Mönch's tutelage before setting up a workshop in his home where he continued to build and study. The energy, which had fueled nightly five-hour practice sessions, was now directed toward learning to construct instruments. He had found his life's passion.

From 1968 to 1970, Jean continued building classic guitars in his home shop before moving into his first commercial space, the second floor of a theater. His work brought him into contact with many people involved with Toronto's thriving folk music community. At their urging, Jean built his first steel string guitar in 1971. They have been primarily a creator of acoustic guitars since the company's inception and to this day produce a limited number of electric guitars.

Just One Electric Guitar

The RS-4 is the end result of four years of craftsmanship and development on the part of Larrivee's masterful team of luthiers. They did not set out to create an electric guitar that could be copied; they began with the desire to create one, and only one, then take that instrument and see how far it could be developed, how far its limits could be stretched to. The core of the guitar is a slim South American mahogany body, overlaid with the industry's thickest, flamed maple carve top (coming in at 3/4" thick). The single piece South American mahogany neck is attached with an extra-long mortise and tenon joint. The Indian rosewood fretboard features a specialty "spoke nut, truss rod" which allows a musician to adjust the truss rod with the strings at tension without a special tool. Two body cutouts add comfort and style to the instrument while reducing weight; the RS-4 weighs in at about eight pounds on average. The RS-4 features Jason Lollar's Imperial Humbuckers, Schaller M6 Tuners & Schaller Strap Locks, LUXE Bumblebee paper-in-oil Capacitors, Switchcraft Switch & Jack, CTS Pots, and vintage Shielded push-back cloth wire.

A New Route

Post 9/11 America saw a dramatic drop in guitar sales. Larrivee had recently completed a move of its facilities to California when the tragic events in September occurred and they were forced to make drastic business decisions in the wake of the disaster. Whereas other companies have gone under or sold themselves off to larger conglomerates, Larrivee shifted its business to focus on higher end guitars, and developed them specifically with only two other lines of guitars. The strategy, at least for this company, paid off as they began to see increased growth in their business and are now just about back on their feet.

Levin

Herman Carlson Levin was born and raised in Åsaka, Sweden. At age 18 he attended carpentry school where he would later garner an apprenticeship with a furniture maker in Gothenburg. In August 1887, Levin moved to the United States and worked for a short time as a carpenter before finding employment in 1888 with a guitar manufacturer.

Three years later he and two partners started a small guitar workshop in New York. He worked diligently and after a brief visit to his homeland in 1895, Levin realized the demand for instruments in Sweden was high and that manufacturing instruments there would be very profitable. So with very little money, Levin opened up "Herman Carlssons Instrumentfabrik" at Norra Larmgatan in Gothenburg.

Little fundage equates to a little space and small staff, just two luthiers. By the close of 1901, 473 instruments were made and in 1903, with a crew of five, Levins 1000th instrument was built. The factory was one of the best in Europe between 1904 and 1912, with Levin receiving several awards including the gold medal in Madrid for best guitar, as well as the Grand Prix Prize.

Steady Improvement for Levin

In the mid-1920s, the plant had made over 50,000 instruments and in 1925, production of a line of banjos was launched. By 1936, the 100,000th instrument had left the plant and Levin was marketing a successful line of archtop guitars. Shortly before 1940, Levin employed a crew of 45 in a much larger facility than where the company had begun 40 years earlier. In the 1950s, Levin launched a line of inexpensive guitars intended for schools and novice guitar players, these guitars were of lower quality than the rest of the Levin line up.

The Inevitable Purchase

In 1952, Jerome Hershman, a guitar distributor from America, noticed a Levin guitar at a trade show in Germany and convinced the Levin company to let them market their guitars in the United States. Hershman knew that the brand name Levin would be hard to market in America and suggested the name Goya which was inspired by the Spanish artist Francisco Goya, who was well known for the guitars that he showed in his paintings.

The Goya line up proved to be successful due to its high quality construction methods. The "Goya brand" was first marketed with Spanish-style nylon string guitars that caught fire (so to speak) with the folk rock movement in the United States. In the late 1950s, a line of steel-stringed flat-tops were launched, with adjustable trussrods and bolted necks.

Goya Departs

The contract was dissolved by Goya Music in 1968, following the acquisition of Goya Music by Avnet Inc, who already at that time owned Guild Guitars. The Goya distribution rights were sold in 1970 to amplifier manufacturer Kustom Electric of Chanute Kansas. In 1972, Kustom went bankrupt and the distribution was taken over by another Chanute company, Dude Inc. It is unclear if Levin ever delivered any instruments to Dude, as the sales made by Dude may have been the remaining stock from the Kustom bankruptcy, which were simply relabeled with a Dude logo.

In 1976 Dude sold the Goya brand to CF Martin who had already purchased the majority of the Levin Company a few years earlier. CF Martin started the import of Japanese and Korean instruments under the Goya name, and both the Goya and Levin brands reputation saw a period of decline. CF Martin stopped offering Goya instruments during the 1990s and sold the brand name in 1999 to Goya Foods.

Line 6

Line 6 got out of the gate in 1996, with the world's first digital modeling guitar amplifier, the AxSys 212. The company underwent a rapid expansion in the early 2000s due to the success of their Pod product line, which isolated modeling circuitry from the AxSys amplifier. Line 6 has become a quiet power in the world of guitar amplification and gearbox design garnering attention from techs and players alike since their creation.

The Pod and other Guitar Gadgets

Modeling technology for musical instruments emulates the sound and nuance of various classic and modern guitar amplifiers, effects pedals, speaker cabinets and microphones, enabling musicians to feed sound reinforcement or recording systems only through the modeling device, optionally eliminating the guitar amplifier as a requirement.

Prior to the development of modeling technology, connection of a guitar and effects directly to a sound system or recording equipment resulted in harsh sounds generally rejected by musicians and recording engineers. Additionally, because the modeling device is digital, thousands of adjustments may be recorded to digital memory and quickly recalled, creating logical possibilities that previously would have been physically impossible during performance. The Pod, designed by Line 6, is one such multi-effects processor that allows the guitar player to modulate his sound without the use of multiple pedals that are connected to a guitar amplifier. The majority of effects processors are PC compatible enabling an easier path to recording sound accurately and more crisply than with an analog signal.

The Chain of an Electric Guitar's Sound

Modeling recognizes that each link in the electric guitarist's chain of electronics contributes to a unique aspect of the resulting sound. Examples of the links in the chain are effects pedals, amplifier, sealed or open speaker cabinets, size, type and quantity of speaker components in the cabinet, microphone type and angle of microphone in relationship to the speaker, and mono or stereo coloration. Complicated? Yes. Modeling can also extend to the instrument itself, with the ability to model various types of acoustic or electric guitars from one guitar, selectable with the change of a multi-position switch. There are many weapons available to the modern guitar player searching for tone. This makes a musician like Jimi Hendrix all the more amazing, who only used two effects in his playing: a Wah-Wah pedal, and "fuzzface" distortion box.

The Pod X3

The Pod X3 or "bean" Pod X3 Live (pedalboard), and Pod X3 Pro (rackmount) products are Line 6's most recent Pod products. They have dual tone capability, more simulations than earlier models, and a variety of effect and output options. Line 6 currently has several other product lines in production, including Spider Valve and Spider III guitar amplifiers, LowDown bass amplifiers, Pod Studio USB audio interfaces and X2 wireless systems. Line 6 is one of the first companies to look to improve their products technology utilizing the internet, having an active user community, and providing software that allows users to easily download and share patches or device settings. This software covers all of Line 6's existing flagship products.

Luna

Yvonne de Villiers was a stained glass artist when she envisioned the guitar company that would become Luna. This inspiration was generated from watching her mother, Hilda, play bass in several bands as she was growing up. Yvonne noticed her mother continually struggle with traditionally heavy electric basses as they weighed down her petite frame. Yvonne reached much the same conclusion that founded Daisy Rock Guitars: women should have guitars designed for their needs. Luna Guitars was founded in 2005, on the principles of creating visually captivating guitars that stimulate the minds and creative spirits of women as well as catering to their unique body design needs to complement their skill sets.

Luna's mission statement is a simple one: "Our focus is on our customers, and we pledge our efforts to serving them responsively," writes Luna Guitars. "We actively encourage their interaction to refine and expand the design of our instrument lines and to influence the development of accessories and services to enhance their guitar playing experiences. We are committed to helping our customers achieve their musical goals and, we embrace the opportunity to contribute to their emotional and spiritual journeys, as well." Luna's artistic creations that continually look to branch out and redefine what art is in the guitar world as well as their continual reinvestment in the environment their working materials come from is testament that they are following their mission statement closely and joyfully.

Gypsy Neo Series

The lightweight and affordable series from Luna offers a Les Paul styled body that is Forest Stewardship Council certified. Built from sustainable mahogany, the Gypsy Neo has a bolt-on neck construction, rosewood fretboard and tune-o-matic bridge. Humbucking pickups give the Neo its bottom heavy sound and allow the electronics to remain light, which allows this electric to weigh slightly more than seven pounds. The singlecut body is available in black or natural finishes.

FSC Certification and its Significance

To earn FSC certification and the right to use the FSC label, an organization must first adapt its management and operations to conform to all applicable FSC requirements. What the FSC rules prescribe is applied globally. This is how FSC makes a positive and permanent impact; at FSC IC a team of experts facilitate the development, review and improvement of FSC rules and procedures.

FSC's standards have been proven to work across continents, forest types, sizes and ownership. The FSC standard-setting process is transparent, democratic and inclusive with many opportunities for the interested public to participate. Their rules in order to obtain certification are as follows: 1. Prohibit conversion of forests or any other natural habitat. 2. Respect of international workers' rights. 3. Respect of human rights with particular attention to indigenous peoples. 4. Prohibit the use of hazardous chemicals. 5. No corruption – follow all applicable laws. 6. Identification and appropriate management of areas that need special protection (e.g. cultural or sacred sites, habitat of endangered animals or plants). Luna is the perfect example of a guitar company doing everything it can do to disrupt the wanton consumption of materials by larger corporations that have milled certain tonewoods (rosewood, mahogany, spruce) to dangerous levels of scarcity.

Left: the Andromeda bass and Paz
Signature bass
Opposite bass: a closer look at the
Henna electric

Manson

Andy and Hugh Manson are luthiers with very divergent and masterful styles. Andy has focused on the guitar as art choosing to work in wood, with acoustics and sculpture producing some of the most interesting creations guitar building has seen for some time. Hugh maintains a shop for building custom electric guitars and features a client roster that holds name like Matt Bellamy, Martin Barre and John Paul Jones.

"A musical instrument is simply a voice for musical ideas," writes Andy Manson, "it can in and of itself inspire music in the way that the voice of a diva moves the songsmith. The beauty of nature's materials and the work of the craftsman combine with the musician in an alchemical event. As in all meetings, the whole is greater than the sum of the parts. As in guitars, the whole is greater than some of the parts."

Hugh Manson's Guitar Designs

The Black Manson was built for Matt Bellamy of the band Muse. A solid body type rests with a bolt-on neck and mahogany body, bird's-eye maple neck, and rosewood fingerboard. A Hot P90 Seymour Duncan pickup rests in the neck position with a Bare Knuckle Mississippi Queen P90 at the bridge position. Hugh designed the Black Manson with a whammy pedal incorporated into the body of the guitar.

"…I looked at the back of a whammy pedal and realized it draws a lot of power," explains Hugh Manson, "unless he wanted a guitar full of batteries that he could only use for 40 seconds, it wasn't gonna work. Then I realised the modern whammy has a MIDI controller system with it, so I went to a great friend of mine, Ron Joyce, who does all my weird electronic stuff, and said, 'I want to control that pedal from this guitar.' He said, 'all you need is a pot.' I looked into pots but realized that rotary pots gave the wrong feel. Eventually we came up with the linear pot from the side of a keyboard, which acts as a MIDI controller pad and goes in to a microprocessor to control the whammy. It just number crunches MIDI numbers -you tell it what you want it to do and it'll do it. It'll control a whammy pedal, it'll control a kaoss pad, it'll turn the lights up and down, it'll turn your heated blanket on, whatever you want in terms of MIDI. I don't think anyone's done that in a guitar before."

The Creations of Andy Manson

The Mermaid Guitar probably stands out as Manson's most dominating piece of art and musical creation in recent memory. A custom built, all wooden statue/acoustic guitar, the Mermaid is a wonderful creation and shows just how far musical instrument building may be taken. Best of all, she plays. The front of the torso, being the soundboard, is carved, inside and out, from Western Red Cedar. The back and arms are of American Cherry, and the scales are of English rippled Sycamore, each piece individually cut and steam bent to fit.

The head, hands and gargoyle are carved from Lime, while the hair and eyelashes are willow and the guitar neck is American flamed maple, laminated with black walnut, cherry and Cuban mahogany, with a fingerboard of bird's eye maple. The guitar head is veneered with figured mahogany and the inlays are of abalone and mother of pearl into bird's eye maple. The Mermaid holds in her left hand a comb of amber, pernambuco and African blackwood, and she wears a pendant of paua shell inlaid into Hawaiian koa. In all 17 kinds of wood were used by Mr. Manson to build The Mermaid - which weighs in at nine pounds. The mermaid was auctioned off in 2006 to benefit the charity Harvest Help.

Below: MB! with a red glitter finish
Opposite page: Andy Manson's
custom built Mermaid guitar

Martin

C.F Martin was born in 1796 in Germany. His predecessors had been cabinet makers and other wood craftsmen, though his father was also a luthier. At an early age Martin's father had him apprenticed to a very well-known guitar maker in Vienna where he trained and learned the craft. Upon completion, C.F returned to his hometown where he set up shop and began to build his own instruments. The guitar at that time in history was the child of the music industry and thought of very little as a classical instrument of any worth. As such it was controlled (as per Europe's guild system at the time) by the cabinet maker's guild. A problem arose when the Violinists' Guild began to claim exclusive rights over the production of musical instruments. They tried three times to litigate away the cabinet maker's right to produce guitars, thrice failing. All the legal warbling soured C.F Martin's taste with the guild system in Europe and he was soon on a ship headed for the North American coast.

By 1833, Martin had moved his fledgling business to the New World, settling at first in New York City, though by 1838 had the company moved to its present day home in Nazareth, Pennsylvania. The Martin Company is generally credited with developing the X-bracing system during the 1850s. Unfortunately or perhaps fortunately C. F. Martin did not apply for a patent on the new bracing system. During the 1850s, X-bracing was used by several makers, all German immigrants who knew each other, and according to historian Philip Gura, there is no evidence that C.F. Martin invented the system. The Martin guitar company was the first to use X-bracing on a large scale, however, and Martin has gone on record as claiming to be the inventors of the "scalloped X-bracing" system of construction as well.

Martin's popularity continued to grow in the 1900s, due to the rise of country western music as well as the continued drive of folk. Country music demanded a louder instrument, and many companies began to shift from an instrument whose strings were made from catgut, to those of steel. C.F Martin & Co. began moving their focus to this type of acoustic guitar by the very early 1920s.

Martin's Electric Offerings

In the late 1960s, Martin manufactured hollow-body electric guitars similar to those manufactured by Gretsch. Martin's electric guitars were not popular (seldom seen by musicians) and the company then decided to continue to concentrate on the manufacture of a wide range of high quality acoustics. They also brought back the famous (and more expensive) D-45 in 1968. In general, Martin's electric guitar creations were not popular and never came close to their acoustic guitar sales.

During the 1960s, many musicians preferred Martin guitars built before World War II to more recent guitars of the same model. The pre-war guitars were believed to have internal bracing carved more skillfully than later instruments, producing better resonance. Additionally, 1960s Martin dreadnoughts suffered from poor intonation in the higher registers. This is attributed by some luthiers and repairmen to a gradual trend of misplacing the bridge on these guitars. Apparently, the same jigs for bridge placement were used throughout the history of each model's production. As the amount of production increased from the Martin factory, the jigs eroded, resulting in inaccurate bridge placement. This was eventually identified and corrected, though not before Martin had already produced a wealth of devalued acoustic instruments. In '79 Martin opened their custom shop that saw the creation of their 500,000th guitar in 1990, the millionth being created 14 years later in 2004.

Maton

Electric guitars from Down Under. Until the mid 1930s, an Australian guitar manufacturing industry was virtually nonexistent. Good quality guitars were hard to find and at this time the best guitars came from the United States. Bill May, a Melbourne-born jazz musician, woodwork teacher and luthier became the catalyst for a musical movement that sought to change all that.

During the early 1940s, Maton established a custom guitar manufacturing and repair business known as "Maton Stringed Instruments and Repairs." This business venture was successful to the point that Bill was able to convince his older brother, Reg, to join him as a full time guitar maker. In 1946, the "Maton Musical Instruments Company" was created.

Maton is still a family owned Australian company, now operated by Linda and Neville Kitchen (Bill May's daughter and son-in-law). Showing great belief in the potential of the company, Bill opened up Australia's first major guitar making facility in Canterbury, Melbourne, in 1949. More than 300 different models were created at the Canterbury factory, a staggering testimony to the creativity of the Maton team from that era. Maton called the Canterbury factory home for 40 years until it was time to upgrade to a more modern and spacious facility in Bayswater, Melbourne, in 1989.

Maton Electric Guitars

Maton has really looked to using woods naturally occurring within Australia and using only a small amount of imports for their guitar designs. Their body styles appear largely proprietary and their popularity is evident by their continued presence in the world as well as the Australian market. The MS500 is built from silver silkwood, and bolted-on quilted maple. Two ceramic (coil-tapped, MVHB and MVSC) pickups are used to provide tone with Jim Dunlop wiring keeping the guitar's quality well in line.

Of the many guitars that comprise Maton's long, well accomplished history, it was the Starline that laid the foundations on which Maton thrives today. Originally produced in the 1940s, the Starline was the flagship model and was highly prized by guitarists of the time. This limited edition reissue is both a fitting tribute to the original guitar as well as the spectacular result of the marriage of traditional guitar making techniques and modern manufacturing.

The Benefit of Perspective

It is difficult to place Maton's success with the rest of the guitar companies building instruments around the world as Maton held sway largely in Australia and Australia alone. They were and are a very attractive option for the local guitar player in that country but it is problematic to say whether or not the company would have succeeded had they been American based and forced to compete directly with giants such as Gibson and Fender.

Right: Ben Harper playing with the Innocent Criminals, Myer Music Bowl, Melbourne Australia

Mirage Guitars was formed in 1973 by Rick Somboretz, to build high-end acoustic guitars. Various electric designs have also been built over the years, and have seen a fair amount of success with collectors and select session guitar players.

Mirage did not start out as an electric guitar producer. The first model Rick created for his would-be company was (of course) an acoustic guitar, the D2. It was first built in 1974 and was intended to be in a batch of some 30 other guitars though the majority of them were never finished. The D2 has had several owners throughout its life and the whereabouts of the other acoustics that Rick created are unknown.

The M6 Electric

What we do know, is that Mirage found its way to creating electric guitars. This instrument produced by Mirage was exhibited at the Dayton Art Institute in 2002 where it received wide praise. The body is made from spalted and figured Ohio hard maple with African ebony. The M6 is built on a 25.5" scale, its arched top and bottom lending comfort to the otherwise wide body. Its electronics are solely up to the purchasing musician as this electric guitar is completely customizable.

The Russian Connection

In 2006, Mirage Guitars founder Rick Somboretz traveled to Russia where he purchased all rights to the Russian King electric guitar series which was originally produced from 1972-1989. "King Strats" as they were called, were built with a slightly wider body than is traditionally acceptable in American electric guitar building, with three single coil pickups, four tone knobs and one selector switch. Mirage now produces these models in an updated, sleeker design.

Michael Kelly

Michael Kelly Guitars is an American guitar, bass and mandolin manufacturer, based in Clearwater, Florida. They are a division of HHI Music Brands, who also own B.C. Rich Guitars. They've been creating quality instruments in their once small shop since 1999. Recently they have gained popularity, particularly due to the greater appeal of the Dragonfly II acoustic bass, which has been used by Duff McKagan, once of Guns 'N Roses, and Shavo Odadjian of System of a Down.

A Moment for the Bass to Shine

For the last four years the Dragonfly models from Michael Kelly have been the most in-demand acoustic basses on the market. The newest version (the third edition) has some important upgrades. Kelly started with a dramatic upgrade in the active amplification system. Now they are built with the Fishman MKAB system, the first pre-amp optimized for acoustic bass. The Dragonfly also features real quilt maple wood on the body. The tone of the maple is brighter, more focused and has added projection. Other upgrades on the Dragonfly 3 is hand scalloped bracing, a double adjustable truss rod and dual graphite reinforcement rods for added neck stability and longevity. Like with all of Michael Kelly's basses, players get improved feel with their 34" scale for the perfect string response. Their vine inlays over the fretboard are also attractive with their dragonfly accent. It is made from authentic pearl and abalone giving the guitar player a bit of pomp in the relegated world of the bass instrument extravagance.

The Hex Series

Returning to the electric guitar we have the Hex Series from Michael Kelly. The Hex X features a flat top with a Michael Kelly tweak; the upper and lower horns are carved like an arch top guitar. The body is built of basswood with a flame maple top. Its rosewood fretboard sits on top of a bolted-on maple neck. Its pickups are Michael Kelly designed PAF-Plus and sit at both the neck and bridge positions. The Hex Dellux model built by Kelly sports Grover Tuners, Floyd Rose Tremolo, and Rockfield Black Betty active pickups.

What Is an Active Pickup?

Pickups can be either active or passive. Pickups, apart from optical types, are inherently passive transducers. Active pickups incorporate electronic circuitry to modify the signal. Passive pickups are usually wire wound around a magnet. They can generate electric potential without need for external power, though their output is low, and the harmonic content of output depends greatly on the winding.

Active pickups require an electrical source of energy (usually one or two 9V batteries) to operate and include an electronic preamp, active filters, active EQ and other sound-shaping features. They can sometimes give much higher possible output. They also are less affected in tone by varying lengths of amplifier lead, and amplifier input characteristics. Magnetic pickups used with active circuitry usually feature a lower inductance (and initially lower output) winding that tends to give a flatter frequency response curve.

The disadvantages of active pickups are the power source (usually either a battery or phantom power), cost, and less defined unique tonal signature. They are more popular on bass guitars, because of their solid tone; most high-end bass guitars feature an active pickup. Most piezoelectric and all optical pickups are active and include some sort of preamp.

Modulus

Modulus Guitars is an American manufacturer of musical instruments, most notably bass guitars built with carbon fiber necks. The company, originally called Modulus Graphite, was founded in part by Geoff Gould, a bassist who also worked for an aerospace company in Palo Alto, California. The name may possibly be from Young's modulus, a measure of stiffness from solid mechanics; carbon fiber has exceptionally high modulus and the brand uses this in contruction.

Electric Guitar Construction Methods

Traditionally, electric guitar and bass necks are made from hardwoods (such as maple or mahogany) reinforced with an adjustable steel "truss rod." Wood, being a naturally occurring material, is prone to variations in density and flexibility. This, coupled with the high stresses created by stretching steel strings across them lengthwise, makes wood necks prone to certain unpredictable and undesirable qualities. Among these are twisting, incorrect "bowing" (either too pronounced or too subtle), and "dead spots," or areas on the neck where notes are quieter or more indistinct compared to other areas. Non-traditional neck materials such as carbon fiber and aluminum are attempts to correct these issues by replacing wood with lighter, stiffer components.

Gould was inspired to experiment with nontraditional materials after attending a 1974 Grateful Dead concert, at which he marveled at the size and complexity of Phil Lesh's heavily modified bass (customized by Alembic) and began to consider the possibilities of lighter, stronger materials. After being passed on by his employers in the aerospace industry, the project of creating hollow, carbon fiber bass necks was brought to fruition by Gould and Alembic, who built a bass with a prototype neck and displayed it at a trade show in 1977. (Immediately after the trade show, the bass was purchased by Fleetwood Mac bassist John McVie). Gould and some of his colleagues in the aerospace industry founded Modulus Graphite and began to make necks for Alembic and other companies before moving on to making entire instruments.

Left: John McVie of Fleetwood
Mac in the recording studio
Circa 1975.
Right: the M92 Graphite Bass

The Role of Bass Guitar

As is often said by music teachers and guitar players throughout the generations, "The bass drives the bus." Modern rock 'n' roll, hip-hop, R&B, and music in general would be nowhere without the bass and the dynamic it brings to a band. Music would have no backbone, and would lack adequate dimension in sound.

The bass player is a persona wrapped in enigma. They are the solitary players, in large part, keeping time for their band and laying the bedrock for their lead guitar player to vamp on continuous solos. The bass line allows the improvising soloist that is the electric guitar, to find its way back to the rhythm section.

Music Man

Ernie Ball was an American businessman, musician, and innovator, widely heralded as a revolutionary in the development of guitar-related products. He began as a club musician on a local television circuit and small business entrepreneur, building an international business in guitars and accessories that would eventually gross $40 million a year in the United States.

Born Sherwood Roland Ball in Santa Monica, California, USA, "Ernie" Ball grew up in a musical family. His grandfather wrote the standard, "When Irish Eyes Are Smiling," and his father was a car salesman who taught Hawaiian steel guitar on the side. Although Ball initially picked up the steel at age nine to please his father, he became bored and gave it up. In his early teens he began to take a renewed interest in the instrument, practicing as many as three hours a day. Within a year he was a member of the Musicians Union.

While still in his early teens, Ball began playing professionally in South Central Los Angeles beer bars. By age 19, he joined the Tommy Duncan Band playing pedal steel guitar. Duncan, the former lead singer with Bob Wills and His Texas Playboys, took the band on tour through the Southwestern United States. During the Korean War, he did a tour of duty in the United States Air Force Band, playing guitar and bass drum. After the military he returned to Los Angeles and continued playing in barrooms and lounges, until landing a job on the 1950s "Western Varieties" program at KTLA television. The position soon gained him wider recognition in the Los Angeles music scene and led to studio work as well as employment teaching music.

The Music Man EVH

The Ernie Ball Music Man EVH is the electric guitar designed for/with Eddie Van Halen. It has been reproduced and renamed many times since its first production run but always under the direct supervision of Van Halen as it is the guitar he plays most consistently on albums and on tour. Music Man produced nearly 6000 of these instruments from 1990-1995, quite a significant amount, but such was the appeal of this iconic guitar player as well as his band.

Van Halen eventually sought greater control and now the electric guitars that bear his name are produced as the EVH Wolfgang. It is composed of a basswood core and AA maple top with a Quartersawn maple neck. A Floyd Rose designed locking nut, and tremolo add to the amenities of the EVH along with its chrome hardware. The Gotoh tuners used on the Wolfgang are EVH branded just as the humbucking pickups it incorporates at the neck and bridge positions are. Another tour-tested feature is the stainless steel fret wire which allows for aggressive play as well as smooth work of the fret hand.

Eddie Van Halen took his electric guitar building one step further than most musicians who have a signature series do: he oversees the production with an entirely separate guitar brand line.

Left: Eddie Van Halen playing a
EVH Van Halen guitar, August 2004

John Dopyera was the first to design the steel resonator guitar in the early portion of the 1900s. He did so at the request of musician George Beauchamp, whose complaint was similar to other musicians of that time period: big bands were drowning his sound out. Beauchamp would go into business with Dopyera to manufacture and distribute the luthier's instruments under the National String Instrument Corporation. Dopyera would leave the company less than a year after it had formed to start the Dobro Manufacturing Company, whose name became the gold standard for steel resonator guitars.

Resonators were produced in two styles: a square-necked style designed to be played like a traditional guitar, and a round-necked style which could either be played as a classical instrument or a lap-steel guitar. One of three main resonator designs are usually built into steel resonator guitars: a single inverted-cone resonator used by the Dobro (made from metal and wooden parts) acoustic, a "biscuit" style cone utilized by National Resonators, and a tri-cone resonator style which was used for the first National Guitars.

Its unique twang and metallic slide notes are the mark of an earlier time when bluesmen roamed the Deep South of America. A resonator is actually still an acoustic guitar, but one whose body is made from one or more metal cones, instead of wood boards that are found with a traditional acoustic instrument. The resonator was the initial answer from luthiers for guitar players who were having trouble being heard over big band instruments like trumpets and trombones. When the amplifier rose to prominence the resonator was mostly abandoned though it still found a home with niche musicians in bluegrass and the blues players of the Mississippi delta.

Electric National Resonators

The Resoelectric has been in production for 19 years and has undergone many changes. In its current model, it features an Audiophile-quality Highlander preamp to mix both the magnetic and piezoelectric pickups. A Jason Lollar designed P-90 pickup is located in the bridge position of the guitar with a Highlander piezo transducer fitted under its saddle. Independent volume controls handle the output of each pickup with a master volume knob controlling them all. The solid mahogany body is capped with a figured maple top bound in ivoroid. Fourteen frets of rosewood are accessible to the guitar player.

The Resonator's place in American (and world) music is just as unique as its sound. Many musicians have remarked that instruments like the Dobro and those produced by National take a lifetime to truly understand the ins and outs of how to get the right tone from them.

Left: the National Airline model from circa 2000
Opposite page: Mark Knopfler playing a National Type-O resonator guitar

Novax

Novax Guitars was founded by Ralph Novak, whose instruments feature frets which are not perpendicular to the instrument's neck (as is standard), but rather fan out at various angles to allow for more comfortable, ergonomic playing and for proper intonation. Charlie Hunter, an acclaimed jazz guitarist, uses Novax guitars extensively, which has helped publicize the brand.

Novax instruments have several unusual design features; these features, while offering an appealing and unique aesthetic, are primarily performance enhancers – yet another feature that shows that these luthiers know what they are doing, and prize sound over looks. Novax has redesigned the guitar to be more playable, more versatile, more in-tune, and more "open" and "alive" sounding. The powerful combination of the Fanned-Fret system coupled to their proprietary individual bridge system results in an instrument with exceptional articulation, a unique tonal signature, and natural playability.

Metaphors and Similes

An appropriate analogy might be found in the evolution of the automobile: until the 1960s, guitars had been like early cars that had carbureted engines and primitive suspension. Makes and models may have look different, but under the hood, they all worked the same (with exceptions in neck construction and pickup selection). Novax guitars are like cars designed with fuel injection and independent four-wheel suspension, though they are still competing in a world that has caught up with them.

How does the Fanned-Fret system work? By combining scale lengths customized for string tension and harmonic response, instruments with greater "fidelity" are possible. A simpler explanation would be "imagine six one-string guitars each with a scale length optimized for the pitch and tone of that string. If a chord was formed by striking all of the one string guitars at once, how might that sound compare to one six-string guitar?" There are several advantages to having this sort of system:

1. Control of string tension across the neck.
2. Adaptability to altered tunings.
3. Increased tuning range (holds tension at higher and lower registers).
4. Even response along the entire neck.
5. Enhanced harmonic definition.
6. Natural, ergonomic feel with an "open" and "alive" tone.
7. It eliminates unwanted non-harmonic overtones.

The NPIB and You

The Novax Proprietary Individual Bridge system contributes to the unique tone of Novax instruments by acoustically isolating each string. Here's how: the continuous metal "base plate" that characterizes most modern guitar bridges allows the saddles to "crosstalk" between strings which makes the tone "muddy." Strings lose their individual harmonic character, or "voice" in a chord. Novak's individual bridge system overcomes this by separating each saddle and "base plate", taking advantage of the natural acoustical damping properties of wood vs. metal. The signature overtone series of each string in a chord remains intact, making the chord sound more "in-tune" and keeping the harmonic interest of the different "voices".

This is seen all working together in Novax's Expression Leopardwood six-string solidbody. The handcarved body sports Bartolini humbuckers and utilizes Novax's proprietary bridge and fanned-fret systems. It is an instrument that appears far and away a unique creation and truly a divergence from the popular body styles and electronics of the day. For the experienced musician, Novax is a delight.

Left: the Novax semi-hollow CH8

Organic

Old world luthiery and modern innovation is the hallmark of Organic. Duncan Wales, master luthier, has built several signature models for the UK based company and they display the finest in both electronic achievement and body style development. Trained at "The Totnes School of Guitar Making," Duncan combines his engineering background with traditional luthier's skills. The Organic Custom is entirely handcrafted, from start to finish, using no automated processes. Custom options are almost limitless, as all Organic Customs are made specifically to order. The Standard and Classic are initially roughed out on a CNC machine, before being completed by hand. This greatly reduces construction time and ensures accuracy.

The Measure of the Materials

Every piece of tonewood that goes into an Organic guitar is personally selected by Wales for its aesthetics, strength, stability and tonal properties. The 5A figured maple tops and headstock veneers are of the highest quality, and are precisely bookmatched. All necks are quarter sawn, and, as with the bodies, are made from one piece of timber. The fingerboards are of the highest quality Macassar ebony, which is beautifully striped. Body, neck and control cover woods are all matched to ensure grain and color continuation. The tonal characteristics of the woods produce rich warm tones, and clear defined highs. Their strength and stability deliver superb response and sustain.

Organic guitars have beautiful natural oil and wax finishes. The tactile beauty of the wood is not buried under layers of lacquer. Instead the natural beauty of the grain is unfilled and exposed. The result is a warm smooth organic texture. Each Organic guitar goes through multiple stages of sanding and polishing (to 12000 grit), before receiving 6 coats of oil and 4 coats of finishing wax. Lacquers can smother the body's vibration and dampen its response, causing high-end loss and general "lifelessness." The Organic guitar's oil and wax finish seals the wood while still allowing for its great feel and excellent tone.

Each organic guitar is precisely set up before leaving the workshop and has a fast low playing action. The Organic Standard, and Classic necks have a slim modern 'C' section with a 16" fingerboard radius. Every fret is hand-fitted, dressed and polished to a mirror finish. The ends of each fret, and the fingerboard edges, are subtly rounded over and polished to produce a wonderfully tactile "played in" feel.

The flowing shape, satin finish with exposed grain, recessed hardware and attention to detail in design and construction, all add up to a truly high quality organic feel.

Left and opposite page: the sensitive treatment of the wood allows it to become a fantastic decoration

Ovation

*Above: members of Lyngstad playing the
Ovation Breadwinner
Opposite page: Mark Bolan and T Rex
playing a Breadwinner*

Ovation as a guitar company has pioneered a new slant in the production of their acoustic guitars. It began in 1966, when aeronautical frontrunner Charlie Kaman unexpectedly revolutionized the instrument. As a longtime guitarist, he understood the needs of players and his extensive helicopter blade experience gave him a better understanding of vibration that most luthiers and guitar manufacturers rarely come across.

Kaman believed he possessed the technology and the know-how to truly create a better acoustic guitar. In 1964, Charlie gathered a small team of aerospace engineers (yes engineers) and set to work improving the instrument. These men were scientists, and went about the problem as men of that ilk would: identifying the issues, researching and solving the problem in a very methodical way. They discovered that the flat back of an acoustic guitar actually hindered the balance and projection. So, these engineers started breaking the time-honored traditions of acoustic guitar construction. Instead of the flat-top or the arch-top, Ovation was the first to create the round-back guitar. Their guitar improved the projection qualities of the instrument, bettered its resonance and balance and gave it a sleeker, more modern look. Two years later the first Ovation rumbled off the production line: The Balladeer.

Ovation has enjoyed a wide array of artist appeal since its creation in the 1960s. Many musicians both famous and otherwise have been attracted to the company's unique body style and customizable amenities. Melissa Etheridge has been a long time Ovation player though there are recent newcomers to the family. Mick Thompson of Slipknot has his own Custom MT37, designed in collaboration with the Ovation team to withstand Slipknot's battlefield-like live shows.

The Ovation VXT

The VXT allows a guitar player to pan from sweet acoustic finger style to hard driving power chords with merely a turn of a knob. A musician may also discover a near infinite range of exciting new sounds by combining electric and acoustic in various amounts. Two Seymour Duncan '59 humbucking pickups supply plenty of electric power to cover a wide range of styles including blues, jazz, country, hard rock and heavy metal.

To provide acoustic realism, the VXT employs Ovation's VIP virtual microphone imaging preamp. This very latest technology offers players access to a natural, studio-quality acoustic sound. The Fishman Power Bridge provides true acoustic attack without Piezo (electric) distortion. The one-piece chambered Honduran mahogany body creates a rich depth for both the electric and the acoustic modes, without a trace of feedback even at high stage volumes. Ovation's hybrid form carries the company's signature headstock and a bit of sex appeal in its sleek body design.

Ovation is a company like Novak and Godin that is really pushing the world of guitar to question its time honored methods, shake them, and find the ability and ingenuity to continue to improve the instrument. Many improvements have been made to the electric guitar since its creation and it appears to be the instrument most willing to accept change between it and the acoustic. Ovation has only just dipped its toes into the "electric guitar" market.

Parker

Parker began his first workshop in Rochester, New York, and produced several critically acclaimed guitar lines, but by 2003 he had sold the company in majority to the U.S. Music Corporation based in Illinois. The infusion of industry capital enabled Parker to open a custom guitar shop in 2005. Ken Parker returned to the company after a seeming hiatus in 2006. He now produces only custom guitar models (to include his arch-tops project) for the company that still bears his name.

As a company, Parker is thought of as an innovator both stylistically and in craftsmanship. Parker guitars are just as easily recognizable as a Gibson, Martin, or Ovation. They have given Ibanez a serious run for their money in the "guitar for the virtuoso" category as well by garnering the reputation of top-notch electronics and tone quality like no other 21st century guitar company.

Parker has continually challenged traditional form with the guitars it has produced both in the electric and acoustic areas of production. They have used composite materials and resin over traditional tone woods and finishes, and where was necessary, Parker looked outside the traditional realm at poplar and basswood. They have also turned to using stainless steel frets as opposed to bone or other materials such as wood and nickel.

The guitar company has also worked to craft ergonomic guitars, ones that are more than easy access granters, but ones that are actually less strenuous to play. Many guitar players have reoccurring shoulder strain from nights on end of touring, or tendonitis from positioning fingers to pluck the right strings. It is great to see a company thinking about the instrument in a broader perspective and one that may not have been so popular 20 years ago.

The Parker Fly

These are the breakthrough guitars that have been chosen by many of the world's finest and most respected players since it was first introduced in 1992. Sleek, balanced, and incredibly responsive, the Parker Fly Deluxe is absolutely unmatched in its range of electric and acoustic sounds. Weighing in at approximately five pounds (most electrics range seven to 10 pounds), it is one of the lightest electric guitars on the market to be full-sized and full-toned.

The body of the Fly is made of carved poplar with a basswood neck. Parker custom-cast aluminum vibrato bridge is employed with stainless steel saddles. DiMarzio custom wound pickups and 3-way mag pickup selection, with push-pull coil tap provide all the necessary artillery a guitar player will require. Custom Fishman piezos and stereo voltage-doubled pre-amp allow the Custom Parker vibrato system to shine.

The DragonFly

It's the first new Parker electric guitar since 2005. The Dragonfly is equipped with all the great features Parker is known for in an elegantly carved new shape, showcasing a new, more traditional and ergonomically shaped upper horn while retaining the look and feel that is unmistakably Parker. The flared headstock provides more strength and allows for a thinner profile and a faster, more comfortable neck. The DragonFly also features a 22-fret fingerboard enabling precise placement of the neck pickup for that classic neck-position tone. An HSS pickup configuration has been utilized for the wider palette of tones that today's guitarists demand from a high end instrument. Pickup mounting has also been improved to allow players to swap out the included Duncans with the pickup of their choice. The DragonFly also marks the first time Parker has combined the premium tone woods of alder and basswood in a production model, further providing a wider range of attainable tones.

Right: a Parker Fly Deluxe
Opposite page and top right:
famous fans of the Parker brand

Paul Reed Smith

Paul Reed Smith is a master luthier and the founder, namesake and owner of PRS Guitars. Originally from Bowie, Maryland, Smith made his first guitar while at St. Mary's College and continued to build guitars after he finished college, making them one at a time at the rate of one a month. Together with another local, John "Orkie" Ingram, they formed the nucleus of what would become Paul Reed Smith Guitars.

Smith would often bring his guitars backstage at concerts to try to do what many other luthiers have, and use rockstar endorsement as a marketing device, and eventually got his break when Derek St. Holmes of the Ted Nugent Band agreed to try out #2, the second guitar Smith had ever made. St. Holmes played the guitar for the first few songs of his set, and Smith told him that after he showed it to some other musicians, he would fly out to Detroit and give it to him.

Smith then contacted Ted McCarty, former president of Gibson and creator of the Explorer, ES-335 and Flying V guitars, for advice on how to approach the guitar industry and essentially "break-in." McCarty would become Smith's mentor and adviser from that day on. The result of their collaboration was the current line of PRS Guitars, which include solid and hollow-body guitars. The Private Stock line of PRS guitars are made utilizing a vast range of exotic materials including various stones, elaborately figured tone woods, and intricate shells for inlays. PRS guitars caught fire in the '90s, when rap/rock and Nu Metal Movements were popularized by bands such as Linkin Park, Drowning Pool and Creed.

Opposite page and below: the McCarty model
Opposite page: (top) Carlos Santana and (below) Alex Lifeson

PRS Moving Forward

PRS Guitars is still based in Maryland and its line of electric guitars now sports several brand lines from McCarty's original (the McCarty II being recently discontinued) creations to the SE, a more affordable make of the PRS look and feel. The Custom 22 and 24 models display the elements that brought such instant popularity for PRS. The Custom 22 has a special 25" scale coupled with a comfortable wide fat neck carve and nickel silver covered PRS Dragon II pickups. The Custom 24 is the core of Paul Reed Smith's line (it's the guitar Paul Reed Smith took to his first trade show in 1985). Today, it still comes with their patented PRS Tremolo bridge, locking tuners, and the beautifully carved, figured maple top that is a PRS hallmark.

Similar in spirit to the double cutaway Mira model introduced at Experience PRS 2007, the single cutaway Starla has many vintage themed appointments and is PRS Guitars' first solidbody electric guitar featuring a standard Bigsby B5 tail piece and a Grover Tune-O-Matic bridge. The guitar also includes exclusive Starla Treble and Bass pickups. The solid mahogany Starla body is accented with a 24" scale rosewood fingerboard, a solid mahogany neck and dot inlays or optional bird inlays. Proprietary Alnico magnets incorporated into the pickup design contribute to the guitar's unique clean and crisp sound but are also capable of rich harmonic overtones when driven. Other features include a uniquely shaped black plastic pick guard, tone and volume pots and a three-way pickup selector.

The Death of Les Paul (1915-2009)

"We lost an icon today, a real musician who never threw in the towel. As an electric guitar innovator, he gave us the fundamental benchmarks on which our industry is built." - Paul Reed Smith.

Peavey

Peavey is a well-deserving pioneer in the manufacturing of musical instruments and amplifiers. Very few guitar shops and large big-box stores are bereft of Peavey's equipment and apparel which has garnered the reputation as being reliable and electronically advanced. The strength of the company has long been their amplification wing with electric and acoustic guitar players alike swearing by their equipment. The guitar, however, has grown on Peavey and they have recently begun to be recognized for their achievements in body style and tone.

Peavey's Electric Guitars Win Awards

The Peavey PXD™ Void III guitar has won the Guitar World Gold Award for Overall Value for its "eviscerating attack" and "infinitely cool" design theme.

"Peavey's new PXD Series Void III is a wicked example of what can be achieved when a company sets out to create a supreme, fully loaded, dominating metal machine," wrote Eric Kirkland in the November 2009 issue of Guitar World magazine. "Every note slammed the front end of the amp, distortion was rampant and harmonics screeched like an eagle on the attack." The Peavey PXD Series is a new breed of extreme electric guitars that captures the aggression and attitude of modern metal players. With supercharged active pickups coupled to menacing slabs of tone-sustaining mahogany, the Peavey PXD Series is the sound of aggression and the perfect complement to the legendary Peavey 6505 Series guitar amplifiers. True to the music that inspired them, PXD Series guitars are built for speed, slicing leads and razor-sharp riffs.

"Peavey's Void III gives true metallists everything they could ever want," wrote Kirkland, "a rock solid Kahler tremolo, a comfortable yet fast neck, active EMGs with hard-hitting ceramic magnets, skeletonized tuning keys, razor-sharp tones and a storm of gain. Metal never gleamed so brightly!" The Peavey PXD Series includes four distinct models, the Void, Tomb, Twenty-Three and Tragic, with a range of feature options including Kahler tremolos, adjustable bridges with a string-through design and wicked body shapes that ship with Coffin Case hard cases or gig bags. PXD guitars feature high-output Peavey VFL™ active pickups or EMG 60 and 81 pickups with the EMG-AB Afterburner tone circuit, which boosts input gain up to 20 dB for the highest levels of saturation.

"True jumbo frets add to the Void III's speed potential and volume, especially for players that utilize legato techniques, tapping and frequent hammer-ons or pull-offs. There's sufficient meat in the mahogany neck's shape to ensure proper resonance, but it's definitely thin enough for vicious shredding." - Peavey

Peavey and Jack Daniels

Jack Daniels and Peavey share a common history as growing from a small, one man operation to a multi-million dollar corporation. It is in that spirit that Peavey has designed a series of guitars bearing the "Old No. 7" seal of approval. The Jack Daniel's Electric EX is a single-cutaway guitar. The Peavey Jack Daniel's electric guitar is constructed from resonant mahogany topped with a custom Jack Daniel's filigree design. The patented Peavey Dual-Compression Bridge system, a string-through-body design, creates a metal-to-metal connection for singing sustain and strong string presence, and two vintage Peavey hum-canceling pickups provide high output and unlimited tone. Chrome machine heads and chrome knobs with Old No. 7 stamped on top add the finishing touch to this special instrument.

Left: the angular Peavey Razer
Right: John Taylor of Duran Duran

Tom Ribbecke has been building and repairing guitars and basses in San Francisco since 1974. He managed to build a reputation for creating instruments that perfectly suit his client's needs and hopes to give a part of himself to every instrument he builds which shows in the breadth and depth of his creative prowess and the time spent on working an instrument to perfection. His shop is almost entirely dedicated to custom instruments and although he offers the option of rejection upon completion no guitar/bass player has ever done so.

Born in Brooklyn, New York, Tom attended NYU Syracuse University Newhouse School of Communications and earned a BFA in Music and a BA in communications. He relocated to San Francisco in the early '70s and opened his first luthiery shop in the Mission district. After 10 years, and thousands of repairs and custom builds for clients, he closed the storefront in order to concentrate on Commission building.

Tom served 10 years with the Association of Stringed Instrument Artisans (ASIA) and as President of the board of directors. His instruments have been featured in the Scott Chinery Blue Guitar Collection for the Smithsonian and in the Boston Museum.

A Guitar Company and a Halfling

Tom Ribbecke has spent his long career perfecting his craft and pushing the limits of design. He developed the Halfling design in 2003 with the help of renowned bass player (and good friend) Bobby Vega. The design is a unique blend of the Steel String/Classical guitar and the Archtop guitar that offers versatility, enhanced bass response and more feedback suppression.

The soundboard of the Halfling is a combination of the flat bass side of a steel string and the arched treble side of an archtop. The instruments are capable of large full fundamental bass response with the ability to hear and distinguish all the notes of a complex chord when ringing together.

This instrument is a unique and proprietary design of guitar or bass that uses the concepts of advanced luthiery design to create a more versatile and efficient stringed instrument. This is done by combining the flat bass side of a steel string or classical guitar top with the carved or arched treble side of the soundboard, to create an instrument that is capable of large full fundamental bass response with the separation of course (ability to hear and distinguish all the notes of a complex chord when ringing together.) In perhaps what could be the continued backlash against larger music stores, guitar players continue to seek smaller and smaller shops looking for that next luthier that's going to push electronics and the art of guitar building to the next plateau of achievement. Ribbecke as a guitar company has been able to produce instruments directly to the guitar player as consumer ensuring that the musician is able to play an instrument (just as Van Halen has his Wolfgang) built to their exact specifications.

Left: a 1864 Ruckenbacker guitar
Top: Serge Pizzorno of Kasabian
Bottom: Peter Buck of REM with a
330 Rickenbacker

The Rickenbacker International Corporation, also known as Rickenbacker, is an electric and acoustic guitar manufacturer, known for being alongside Gibson and Fender as a company with one of the most imitated body styles in guitar making. All production takes place at its headquarters in Santa Ana, California. Rickenbacker is the largest guitar company to manufacture all of its guitars within the United States.

The company was founded as the suspiciously-named Ro-Pat-In Corporation (ElectRo-Patent-Instruments) by Adolph Rickenbacher and George Beauchamp in 1931 to sell electric "Hawaiian" guitars which had been designed by Beauchamp, helped by his fellow employees at the National String Instruments Corporation, Paul Barth and Harry Watson. For these guitars, they ultimately chose the brand name Rickenbacher (later changed to Rickenbacker), though early examples tend to have an Electro brand name on the headstock. These instruments, nicknamed "frying pans" due to their long necks and circular bodies, are the first solid-bodied electric guitars, though they were not standard guitars, but a lap-steel type. They had huge pickups with a pair of horseshoe magnets that arched over the top of the strings. By the time production ceased in 1939, several thousand frying pans had been produced.

From their inception, Electro String also sold amplifiers to go along with their electric guitars. A Los Angeles radio manufacturer, Mr. Van Nest, designed the first Electro String production-model amp. Shortly thereafter, design engineer Ralph Robertson was hired to further develop the amplifiers and by the 1940s, at least four different Rickenbacker amplifier models were made available. James B. Lansing of the Lansing Manufacturing Company designed the speaker in the Rickenbacker professional model. During the early 1940s, Rickenbacker amps were sometimes repaired by fellow Californian Leo Fender whose repair shop soon evolved into the Fender Electric Instrument Manufacturing Company.

Rickenbacker Made Famous

In Hamburg in 1960, the then-unknown John Lennon bought a 325 Capri, which he used throughout the early days of The Beatles. He eventually had the guitar's natural alder body refinished in black (a color later to be officially known as 'Jetglo' by Rickenbacker), and made other modifications including the fitting of Bigsby tailpiece and regularly changing the knobs. In its final modified form, Lennon played this guitar during The Beatles' famous 1964 debut and third appearance on "The Ed Sullivan Show."

A brand new one-off custom 12-string 325 model was created just for Lennon and was shipped to him (along with a second 6-string model) while The Beatles were in Miami Beach, Florida, on the same 1964 visit to the U.S. He used this newer model on The Beatles' sequentially "second" appearance on "The Ed Sullivan Show" which was broadcast live for the East Coast and simultaneously taped to time for same-day broadcast to the other U.S. time zones.

Lennon accidentally dropped the second 325 model during a 1964 Christmas show, breaking the headstock which made the instrument go hopelessly out of tune every time he played it. While it was being repaired, Rose Morris, the official UK importer of Rickenbacker at the time, gave Lennon an export version of the 325 called the 1996. Lennon later gave it to fellow Beatle and friend Ringo Starr. Fear that the guitar had been destroyed in a 1979 fire at Starr's Los Angeles home was laid to rest in 2005, when Starr and his lead guitarist used it on a recording. Ringo owns this Rickenbacker to this day.

In 1963, George Harrison of The Beatles bought a 425 during a brief visit to the U.S. In February 1964, while in New York City, F.C. Hall of Rickenbacker gave Harrison the second prototype model OS 360/12 FG electric 12-string Rickenbacker ever made. This instrument became a key part of The Beatles' sound on "A Hard Day's Night" and other Beatles songs through late 1964, and was played by Harrison throughout his life.

Robin

The Best Television Appearance Ever

The founder of Robin guitars was inspired in his childhood – in the summer of 1964 to be precise. Someone said "Come and see what's on tv" and his life was changed forever, together with literally millions of other kids and teenagers in America and around the world. The Beatles on "The Ed Sullivan Show" forced the electric guitar into the limelight – some would say that it was the first time that the electric guitar was truly noticed. Afterwards, David Wintz claims that he remembers drawing pictures of electric guitars on his notebook in the sixth grade, before he even realized what an electric guitar was supposed to look like.

The electric guitar craze took over his hometown (and most of the US) fairly quickly and suddenly being in a garage band was the desire of every teenage boy in America. The instruments these boys played are now sought after by collectors the world over.

Wintz's true awakening, however, came when he visited a vintage guitar show in Houston. "This place was a funky lowdown hole in the wall full of what most people at the time would have considered junk. I think at that moment I was lost to the guitar as a piece of art, as much or maybe ever more so than actually playing it". Within a month, Wintz became obsessed with buying used and vintage guitars, and he spent every spare moment hunting or playing them.

Within that year he teamed up with a friend to form what would become Houston's 'oldest and longest running guitar shop' to date. During the following 10 years, they became known as the source of repairs, refinishing classic instruments in the Texas Gulf Coast area, and trading and repairing thousands of guitars from acoustic and electric manufacturers, both in the U.S. and abroad.

Eventually, the friends' attention turned from trading to creating guitars, which was a radical change but the need to always customize, restore and push for better design and higher quality remained the cornerstone of Robin Guitars. After experimenting, as many manufacturers did, with foreign production, Robin decided that the only way to retain the quality of their guitars was to bring production back to the U.S. A decision that was made easier with the 1987 fall of the dollar against the yen, making production more costly but with the same quality.

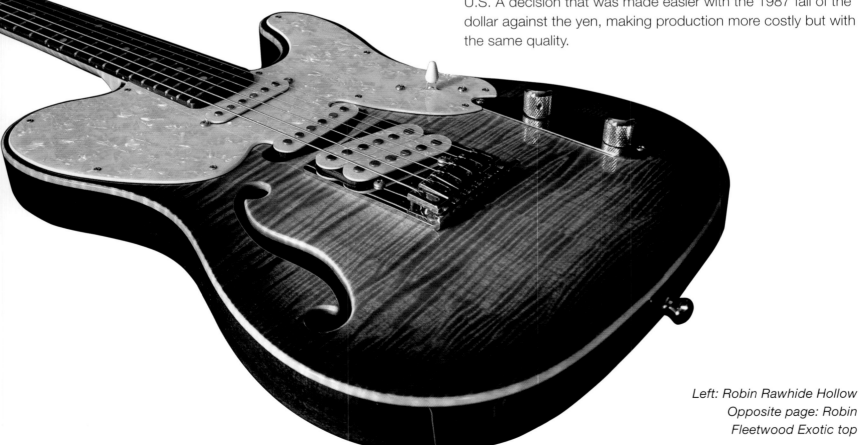

Left: Robin Rawhide Hollow
Opposite page: Robin
Fleetwood Exotic top

Schecter Guitar Research, commonly known simply as Schecter, is an American guitar manufacturer. The company was founded in 1976 by its namesake David Schecter and originally produced replacement parts for existing guitars from manufacturers such as Fender and Gibson and not the guitars themselves. Today, the company mass-produces its own line of electric guitars, bass guitars, and steel-string acoustic guitars.

In the Beginning...

David Schecter opened Schecter Guitar Research in 1976, this was a repair shop in Van Nuys, California and not a research facility, as the name might suggest. The small repair shop manufactured replacement guitar necks and bodies, complete pickup assemblies, bridges, pickguards, tuners, knobs, potentiometers, and miscellaneous other guitar parts for big brand guitars. Eventually, Schecter Guitar Research offered every part needed to build a complete guitar. It supplied parts to big guitar manufacturers such as Fender and Gibson, and to custom repair shops that were building complete guitars out of Schecter parts, so they only needed to assemble the parts (which, obviously, were all compatible). By the late 1970s, Schecter offered more than 400 guitar parts, but did not offer any finished instruments.

Who Are You?

In September 1979, Alan Rogan, then guitar tech for Pete Townshend of The Who, picked up a custom shop Schecter guitar. It was a Fender Telecaster-style guitar with two humbucking pickups and a Gibson Les Paul-style pickup selector. Townshend immediately fell in love with it, and it became his main stage guitar. He later had several similar instruments built from Schecter parts and assembled by Schecter and U.K. based guitar maker Roger Griffin. Townshend last used a Schecter on stage at The Who's 1988 appearance at the BPI Awards Show, although Simon Townshend, Pete's brother and part of The Who's touring band since 2002, continues the relationship between the band and this brand and often plays one of these guitars during Who concerts.

By 1983, Schecter had reached its custom shop production limit and could no longer meet demand. That year, the company was purchased by a group of Texas investors who wanted to build upon Schecter's reputation for quality. The investors moved the company to Dallas, Texas, where they produced quality guitars under the Schecter name for less than five years.

Just a year later, at the winter NAMM show, Schecter introduced 12 new guitars and basses, all based on Fender designs. The most popular of these guitars was a Telecaster-style guitar similar to those that Pete Townshend played. Although Townshend never endorsed this model, it was known unofficially as the "Pete Townshend model." Eventually, the Telecaster-style guitar became known as the Saturn, and the company's Stratocaster-style guitar became known as the Scorcher.

Buyouts and Mergers

In 1987, the Texan investors sold the company to Hisatake Shibuya, a Japanese entrepreneur who also owned the Musicians Institute in Hollywood and ESP Guitars, however ESP and Guitar Research have always remained separate entities. Shibuya moved the company back to California and returned Schecter to its custom shop roots, devoting all its efforts to manufacturing high-end, expensive custom instruments. Schecter guitars were once again only available from a few retailers, one of them being Sunset Custom Guitars located in Hollywood, which Hisatake Shibuya also owned. Sunset Custom Guitars was where Michael Ciravolo, the future president of Schecter Guitar Research, worked.

In 1995, Schecter introduced the S Series guitars and basses, which were Fender-style instruments with an average price of $1,295. In 1996, Hisatake Shibuya asked Michael Ciravolo to become Schecter's president and run the company. Michael Ciravolo, an experienced musician, brought to the company many well-known musicians as endorsees. Musicians are the single greatest marketing tool available to any guitar company.

Opposite page: the Schecter S Series in a variety of finishes

Silvertone

Although Sears and Silvertone have not been associated for over 30 years, a great proportion of the public still associate them with each other. The success and reknown of the Sears-Silvertone brand has meant that their association lives on far longer than the brand itself! The radio and guitar in particular are highly collectible items and are largely responsible for America's fond recollection of the Sears-Silvertone collaboration.

Story Time

In 1915, Sears introduced the Silvertone phonograph, a hand-cranked machine that could be purchased as freestanding or tabletop versions. All phonographs came with a two-week, money-back guarantee. Sears began selling Silvertone radios in the early 1920s, soon adding Silvertone radio tubes and batteries to the product line but it was not until the 1930s that their popularity erupted and they became an item found in so many households. The era corresponded with the outbreak of military aggressions in the Pacific theater. With the approach of World War II, the requirements for radios changed as people bought them as a means to stay updated on the progress of the war, and not just for home entertainment.

Today, the Internet is filled with pages of Sears Silvertone radio collections and information about the antique radios. Their designs, particularly the stylish use of plastic casing, continue to be very popular among radio collectors.

Silvertone Musical Instruments

The Silvertone name replaced the Supertone brand on musical instruments in the 1930s. Struggling blues musicians of the 1940s and 1950s first popularized the Silvertone guitar, with legends such as Muddy Waters and Arthur "Big Boy" Crudup among those who played Silvertones.

The Sears Silvertone guitar was able to make its mark in music history as the unofficial "first guitar" of guitar's icons – setting the trend of celebrity and rock star endorsers for decades to come. Chet Atkins, Bob Dylan and Jimi Hendrix, among many others, played their first chords on a Sears-Silvertone. Sears' guitars have even been immortalised by their mention in songs from artists as diverse as Mary Chapin Carpenter and G. Love and Special Sauce.

Thanks to their solid construction and inexpensive pricing, Sears-Silvertone guitars gained massive popularity among younger musicians. Their legacy lives on today as literally hundreds of stories filled with fond recollections from people of their first guitar, the Sears Silvertone. As with the Silvertone radio, Sears Silvertone guitars are considered prized pieces of many guitar collections, particularly models such as the 1963 "amp-in-case" guitar, which featured an amplifier built into the guitar's carrying case.

Many other musical and audio items bore the Silvertone brand name, but the guitar and radio remain the most popular and fondly remembered, possibly due to the communal nature of these items. Sears introduced a Silvertone record label in the 1920s, which represented many of the era's most popular recording artists. In the 1950s and early 1960s, the Silvertone brand name appeared on all Sears electronic equipment as the companies made the most of their popularity and diversified to sell console televisions, tape recorders, walkie-talkies, radio batteries, hearing aids and car radios.

By the end of the 1960s, the Silvertone brand name was taken from a lot of these items and only appeared on musical instruments and the top-of-the-line stereo equipment and televisions. Silvertone products last appeared in the spring 1972 catalog on televisions and stereo systems.

Left: the 14481 Amp in Case
Opposite page: Beck performs in Portugal

Slingerland guitars were made by Henry Slingerland who began his career working for a company that printed ukelele instruction books. With time and further business success, Henry bought The Chicago Correspondence School of Music from its previous owner in 1914 and changed its name to the Slingerland Correspondence School of Music.

The Slingerland company initially sold ukuleles imported from Germany, eventually making the move from trading to production of ukuleles, banjos, and – with time – guitars in 1923. The Slingerland company indeed proved to have a long history with name and product line specialization changes.

Banjos, the Wave of the Future

In 1928, when Slingerland's success as a drum manufacturer was coming to a head, Henry Slingerland changed the company name from the "Slingerland Banjo Company" to the "Slingerland Banjo and Drum Company", inkeeping with the new production. The Slingerland Company proved itself by the end of the '20s as the world's largest family-owned drum manufactuers – hence the company's name matched its profile and dominant market share. The company's name was changed again sometime during the 1930s to "The Slingerland Musical Instrument Mfg. Company."

Focusing on the actual vintage Slingerland guitar history, most literature has it that the first known commercially produced Spanish solid body electric guitars came along sometime between 1936 and 1939, and was the Slingerland guitar model 141, while model 140 was reserved for the lap steel guitars.

As with many brands of that period, there has been a degree of controversy surrounding the origin of the designs – did Slingerland design the guitars himself or 'borrow' the ideas from other guitar designers when he registered the shapes under the well know Slingerland and May Bell names. For instance, Les Paul (1940), Paul Bigsby and country singer Merle Travis (1947) and others were known to be experimenting with or designing solid-body guitars that resemble those in the market today.

Before ceasing guitar production completely at the beginning of World War II, there were doubts surrounding the Slingerland guitar origin. They did not have the distribution network that other manufacturers boasted, and never promoted these instruments in the same way that they did the drums and banjos.

If it wasn't the Slingerland company that designed and built the "Slingerland" or "May Bell" trademark guitars, then who did? This is another controversial issue. Many experts tend to believe that Harmony and/or Regal were the actual sources. Nevertheless, we could never conclude for certain that the Slingerland company only had the benefit of producing the guitars under trademark names rather than also being the source of some of their original designs. However, as far as what it is today about the Slingerland guitar, it is a brand name rather than an original model made by Mr. H. H. Slingerland himself.

Squier

Squier was acquired by Fender (owned in turn by CBS) in 1965 when it bought an American-based string-making company, but they did not use this part of their acquisition for years. Prior to the introduction of the Fender Squier series of 1982 the lower-end Fender instruments, such as the Lead Series, were made in their Californian plant, which did not include reproductions of their timeless Stratocaster or Telecaster designs.

Cheaper Japanese reproductions in the '70s and '80s, however, forced Fender to come up with a new strategy, as they were struggling to compete with the Japanese-made instruments that were enjoying increasing popularity thanks to their price-tag. In the early 1980s the production costs of these Japanese replicas were far lower than those in America, which forced the price of the original models up – Fender, as a result, exported production to Japan.

American sales were not the only ones that Fender was struggling with – Japanese brands such as Greco and Fernandes were overtaking Fender sales in Japan by quite a large margin. The movement of production, therefore, benefited Fenders in Japanese and international which had been lagging in these countries due to numerous law suits over patent infringement – the Japanese manufacturers reinvented themselves to avoid further cases which resulted in greater competition for Fender.

Fender's negotiations with various Japanese distributors yielded an agreement with Yamano Gakki and Kanda Shokai. Gakki are also known for being part of Epiphone Japan and Shokai owned the Greco brand name; one of the conditions of their contract with Fender was that they cease production of Greco Fender copies. This agreement was mutually beneficial since Fender removed their much cheaper competitions, and Shokai would distribute Japanese Fender guitars in Japan. However, there was a breakdown in negotiations and Gakki was chosen instead.

The first Squier series was launched in July/August 1982 and over time the Squier series has slowly evolved to include original model designs and production has moved from Japan to various other Asian countries such as Korea and China.

Squier Models Outside the Fender Scope

There have been a few Squier models that have been distinct enough in specification from standard Fender models to be notable, such as the Super-Sonic, the Squier '51 (a design that hybridizes elements of the Stratocaster, Telecaster, and 1951 Fender Precision Bass), and the Jagmaster (partially derived from the Fender Jazzmaster and Jaguar). The Bullet name, currently used for an inexpensive Stratocaster variant, was originally applied to an early '80s short-scale model which resembled a hybrid of a Strat and a Mustang.

There are also original and distinct editions of existing Fender guitar designs like the Fender Stratocaster and Fender Telecaster, such editions being the Hello Kitty Stratocaster with pink finish and fingerboard inlays and the Hello Kitty logo, the OBEY Graphics series of Stratocasters and Telecasters with custom handpainted bodies or the Avril Lavigne and Eric Clapton editions. Most of the variation in these models comes in the decoration, rather than body shape or electronics.

Opposite page: (left) Squier Classic Vibe Stratocaster and (right) the Squier J5 Telecaster

Stagg

Established in1995, Stagg is a brand dedicated to bringing high quality musical instruments and accessories to musicians of all types, at the most attractive prices. All of their instruments are handmade from designs created by their team of specialists at their global headquarters in Belgium.

The company's full range of instruments covers everything from brass and woodwind, guitars and bass, drums and pro audio, as well as a wide array of musical accessories. Stagg instruments are available all over the world through their extensive distribution network. If a large part of any guitar company's success is being able to find them, Stagg does not have such an issue. They are constantly changing and evolving their product line to bring the musician the widest choice and the best quality they are able to provide.

Stagg Instruments

Body style designs are somewhat lacking at first glance from Stagg with several lines being dead ringers for Gibson SG's and Les Pauls. The R-Series though offers some break from the pilfering of form to show how Stagg is able to create their own unique look and provocative sounding equipment.

The R500-GBK looks a little similar to the Shecter body design but provides enough difference as to not be immediately noticeable. Humbucking pickups and locking tremolo round out its sleek features that make this Stagg electric one the highlights of its guitar line.

Stagg's "heavy" series is split into three categories of varying body styles carved up from various already established guitar companies. What this shows is that at the very least the problem of body style "pirating" on the part of guitar companies is not solely isolated to the island of Japan. European companies do this just as often as Asian ones, though apparently with a far smaller degree of scrutiny than those in the Far East.

Stromberg

For eight years Stromberg Jazz Guitars' goal has been to present an archtop guitar that will bridge the gap between the recent glut of mass-produced, over-hyped factory guitars and the high end hand built instruments by creating an instrument that does not compromise it's craftsmanship and materials in favor of wide distribution, but also is not so esoteric that only rockstars can gain access to them. The result is a series of playable, and readily affordable guitars that are made with traditional materials but utilizing all that modern technology has to offer.

The Montreaux, Monterey, and Newport

This jazz guitar built by Stromberg has a multi-layered laminated binding on the binding and neck. Its sides and back are maple with its top being built of laminated spruce. Its pickguards are custom made in the United States and owe much of their sustain and tone to two Kent Armstrong Vintage Jazz humbuckers.

Construction methods are similar on the remaining two archtop models with a few differences. The top, sides, and back of the Monterey is of flame maple, with its pickups being Kent Armstrong P-90 humbuckers. The Newport features a side-mounted Kent Armstrong Jazz Slimbucker with hidden volume control.

The archtop in and of itself is not a complete electric guitar and owes much of its roots to the acoustic. The hybrid aspects of its form have been appealing to many guitar players seeking a path back to where they came from stylistically as well as tonally. It was these guitars (introduced in popular fashion by Gibson in the 1930s) that created the competitive atmosphere that would eventually lead Leo Fender, Les Paul and several others to ponder what a guitar would sound like when completely electrified.

Right: the Stromberg Newport non-cutaway

Suhr

Suhr Guitars has a longstanding reputation for being a very fine producer of musical instruments. They believe the "… produce dreams that inspire musical passion and artistic creativity. Our fervent dedication to the highest quality standards possible, our famous fanatical attention to detail, our ears for tone, and our love for music ranging from rock to country to jazz to blues to pop to metal to fusion are all evident in every instrument we produce." Suhr guitars claim to be manufactured with the intention of creating the very best instruments possible, led by the vision of their founder, John Suhr.

Small Workshop, Modern Facility

Suhr Guitars is a complete facility where the entire process of guitar making takes place – from conception, to design right through to finish. Suhr cut their own guitar necks, bodies and pickguards on their state-of-the-art CNC (Computer Numeric Control) routers. Each guitar is detailed prior to paint and assembly - this allows them complete control over quality and consistency of their guitars. These are truly hand-built guitars, each assembled by one builder – an unusual feature for modern guitar construction. However, the desire to maintain the luthier's relationship with each instrument does not necessitate the rejection of technology – guitar makers make the most of computer aided design and construction to finish their guitars to the highest specs possible.

"Suhr's paint process ensures that the beauty of the wood shines through and contributes to the tone of the instrument. Tight neck fits, accurate string alignment and consistent friendly neck back shapes are considered a de facto standard that Suhr replicates in every guitar they build." – Suhr Guitars

John Suhr, the Man

John's building career started, as many others do, with the search for the perfect tone. He began building his own instruments 35 years ago in New Jersey and quickly found a job working for Rudy Pensa at Rudy's Music Shop in New York. This first job led to the formation of Pensa-Suhr Guitars, which built instruments for Mark Knopfler, Eric Clapton, Lou Reed, Chuch Loeb and Robert Palmer, among others.

Feeling the need to move on, John left New York in 1991 to nurture his interest in tube amp design by working with Robert Bradshaw to design CAA 3+ and 3+SE tube preamps. Four years later, John returned to his original vision and began working as a Senior Master Builder at the Fender Custom Shop.

Right: Mark Knpfler playing his Suhr / Schecter Stratocaster guitar

Takamine

Above: Garth Brooks performs onstage at the Dream Concert presented by Viacom at Radio City Music Hall on September 18, 2007 in New York City

Takamine takes its name from the mountain that the company's headquarters is built at the foot of in Sakashita, Japan. Takamine Guitars has more than 40 years of history dedicated to innovation and improvement to the art and craft of guitar making. What first began as a small family business has evolved into one of the leading guitar manufacturers in the world, depended upon by some of the best players and biggest names in the music industry. In order to understand Takamine's development and growing popularity, we will need to go back to 1960s Japan. That is a time when playing the guitar and its greatest vehicle for the people, rock 'n' roll, was becoming popular. As more people wanted to take up the instrument, the need for more guitars obviously increased. Takamine started manufacturing guitars during this time period, largely to meet these needs.

Demand only increased for quality guitars and Takamine met it head on, growing their business in the process. As a result of this, they hired Mr. Mass Hirade in 1968 to add skill and creative talent to their design team. They needed someone who could help develop and create guitars that would appeal to the changing musical tastes of the nation. One of his biggest contributions was the development of their (Japanese) Classical model, a guitar that achieved great popularity among those in Japan.

Takamine is known for two things: the quality of their instruments (Hirade played a big part in this) and their prices. They have an excellent budget line of guitars that has also achieved some popularity because even though they are inexpensive, they are known to have good quality.

There are no pure "electric" guitars produced by Takamine as they would pertain to this history. That is not to say that Takamine has no place with the electric guitar, quite to the contrary. Acoustic/electrics have grown massively in popularity since the crossing over of mainstream country artists such as Garth Brooks and Kenny Chesney, and are favorites of musicians who wish to play large venues where an acoustic instrument may not be the best choice.

Innovations in Pickup Design

Takamine made great advancements with their palethetic pickup. This proprietary piece of equipment featured a clear, clean tone which complimented the acoustic guitar well and

lent itself easily to electrification. With individually shielded six piezo-electric transducers, one for each string, the unit is hanged down and right beneath the bridge saddle. This unique design allows the pickup to be isolated from the vibration of the body, and enables each transducer to pick up the vibration of the string directly through the bridge saddle, which contributes to realizing unmatched levels of anti-feedback even under mega-volume environment. This in-house system of electronics is indicative of guitar companies as a whole and it is interesting to see acoustic workshops that are "cut off" from the rest of the world market for several years innovating in similar ways as those companies that are not.

Taylor

Taylor Guitars has the rare distinction of being a guitar company which is still owned and operated by the person that founded it. Bob Taylor, a luthier that started in the business of guitar making at the age of 18, is still his own master many years later, at the helm of the company he helped create with Kurt Listug. The company is based in El Cajon, California.

Their beginnings were rough and lean. Taylor scratched hard to make a living in the early days of the company, working in a damp warehouse that was barely more than a swamp. How Taylor Guitars survived is a story of will and passion, elements integral when creating something that will carry a life of its own into the world. Taylor and Listug have made musical-instrument history by becoming the first American luthiers in this century to take an acoustic guitar company from one-off shop to production-level manufacturer without relinquishing ownership or creative control.

"But it was fun. What did we know? We were just kids. Somehow, we'd skirted having to get real jobs. We didn't have a boss, we were making guitars. What could be better?" – Bob Taylor

As a 17-year-old, he had seen a 12-string acoustic guitar in a local store window, and, lacking the funds to purchase it, had decided to make his own. He built three guitars while still in high school, working on them at night in the back of a service station, in between filling gas tanks and wiping windshields. Eventually, Taylor took his finished instruments to Sam Radding at American Dream. Radding was convinced that he had a future in the trade.

During their first year at American Dream, Taylor and Listug made a few guitars, but mostly did repairs. When Radding decided to sell the business in 1974, the employees split into rival purchasing groups of two, each team jockeying for position while trying to figure out how to come up with the requisite capital. Finally, a triumvirate of Taylor, Listug, and Schemmer bought the American Dream. Euphoric with ambition, they renamed it the Westland Music Company.

The Standard Electric

Taylor's solid body electric was designed entirely from the ground up and features their own, in-house built humbuckers, bridge, tone controls and body aesthetic. No matter how far a guitar player might push it, this guitar has established durability.

The Standard closely follow the solidbody designs of Gibson's more iconic rock creations but with several Taylor tweaks in production. Taylor's humbucking pickups are what spawned the idea for the Standard Electric and give this guitar much of its growl and bite. These new humbuckers called for something more substantial than an arched top or an acoustic, so the solidbody was the next logical choice.

The Ups and the Ups

"Those first guitars had some structural problems, and sometimes the backs would ripple," Listug recalls, "we knew they couldn't compete aesthetically with the best guitars on the market, so we just kept working at it until we had a marketable-looking guitar."

While they could sell their prototypes in the workshop, the partners had their sights set higher and decided to take their wares directly to dealers in Los Angeles. In 1976, they loaded up their van and did just that. "They liked them, and I actually came home with checks in my hand," Listug says. The genuine candor of Listug's recollections shows the character of Taylor Guitars as a whole. They were a couple of kids with a dream that took a chance on doing what they loved. While this doesn't always work out, it is a plan that has come to fruition enough times that people believe that hard work pays off. And…a little luck.

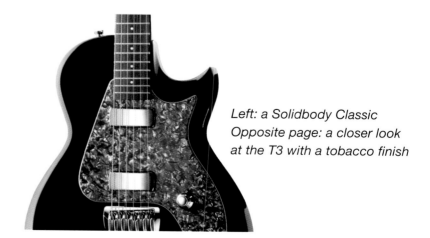

Left: a Solidbody Classic
Opposite page: a closer look
at the T3 with a tobacco finish

Born in La Cañada de San Urbano, Almería, Antonio de Torres was the son of Juan Torres, a local tax collector, and Maria Jurado. His family encouraged him to take an apprenticeship with a master carpenter in the hope that he could assume that business.

In 1833, a dynastic war broke out, and Torres joined the army as a conscript but was dismissed as medically unfit for service thanks to some maneuvering on the part of his father. As only single men and widowers without children were being drafted, his family pushed Torres into a hastily arranged marriage to the 13-year-old daughter of a shopkeeper to avoid having to fight. So, in 1835 Antonio wed Juana María López. Children soon followed: a daughter in 1836, and another in 1839, a third in 1842 who died a few months later. His second daughter also died. And, in 1845 his wife died at the age of 23 of tuberculosis. These years put a strain on Torres, he was often in debt and always looking for more lucrative employment.

The Tutelage of Torres

Although there is some debate as to who taught Torres, the predominant theory is that around 1842, Torres may have gone to work for José Pernas in Granada, continuing his previous education in luthery. He soon returned to Sevilla, and opened a shop on the calle Cerrageria No. 7 which he shared with Manuel Soto y Solares. Although he made some guitars during the 1840s, he only made guitar making his profession in the 1850s thanks to the advice of Julián Arcas, a guitarist and composer at the time. Julian Arcas offered Torres advice on building, and their collaboration increased the confidence and quality of Torres' building. Torres reasoned that the soundboard was key. To increase its volume, he made his guitars not only larger, but fitted them with thinner, hence lighter soundboards that were arched in both directions, made possible by a system of fan-bracing for strength. These bracing struts were laid out geometrically, based on two triangles joined at their base creating a kite shape, within which the struts were set out symmetrically. This created fantastic strength, since the triangle is geometrically the strongest shape to build with; while Torres wasn't the first to use this method he was the one who perfected the symmetrical design. In a bid to prove that it was the top, and not the back and sides of the guitar that gave the instrument its sound, in 1862 Torres created a guitar with back and sides made entirely of papier-mâché. (This guitar is now in the Museu de la Musica in Barcelona. Unfortunately it is no longer

playable). Another of his experiments --perhaps a better description would be a display of his craftsmanship-- was a guitar made like a Chinese puzzle that could be assembled without glue, and when taken apart could fit in a shoe box.

Notes and Quotes

Torres was a secretive man, and so had no apprentices or fans to speak of, but in a letter to his friend Juan Martinez Sirvent explained:

"My secret is one you have witnessed many times, and one that I can't leave to posterity, because it must with my body go to the grave, for it consists of the tactile senses in my finger pads, in my thumb and index finger that tell the intelligent builder if the top is or is not well made, and how it should be treated to obtain the best tone from the instrument."

Torres Guiars now manufactures amps and electrics for themselves and other companies.

Traveler

The name of Traveler Guitars describes exactly what they do – they create travel guitars, both full-scale electric and acoustic, and have been the leading manufacturer of these instruments since 1992 thanks to innovation in their designs and solutions for various types of players. The focus of their instruments is that they have to be lightweight, portable and extremely durable for the travelling player, but they create electric, acoustic, nylon and bass instruments that fulfill this ideal so, unlike some other similar companies, their aim does not limit their designs.

Escape MK-II Steel

The release of the Escape series in 2003 exceeded the expectations of both purists and existing Traveler Guitars fans, so Traveler lifted the bar once again in 2007 with the Escape MK-II line. The updated Escape line still includes a full-scale steel string, classical, and bass model. Traveler Guitar consulted with John Carruthers to improve the ergonomics of the Escape line – their collaboration with this innovative guitar builder has made this series feel more like a traditional guitar than ever before. Not only has the body been updated, but the new MK-II also boasts a custom Element-Hybrid pickup system from L.R. Baggs. All three models come equipped with the system which has onboard electronics with a 2-band EQ, a built in headphone amplifier, and like all Travelers, the ability to be plugged directly into a traditional amplifier for live applications. The entire Escape MK-II line features classic finishes with elegant binding and ebonized fingerboard.

The Speedster

The Traveler Speedster is the electric evolution in Turner's original Pro-Series model. Known best for its attractive retro design and removable "teardrop" upper arm support, this full 24" scale guitar is ideal for the electric player. 2007 marks the transition from the Speedster's original machine-turned-aluminum accents to an updated chrome, giving the guitar a bold new look. The 22-fret Speedster comes packed with a high output dual blade humbucker, a fully adjustable bridge and the look, feel and sound of a full body electric. Smart engineering gives the Speedster its remarkable tone and sustain, which you will have to hear to believe. Whether a musician is playing lead or rhythm, the Speedster is the ultimate compact traveling companion both on the road and on stage.

Escape EG-1

In early 2006, Traveler Guitar was busy at work updating the Escape line for 2007 when one of Traveler's engineers suggested that they make contact with the internationally recognized guitar builder John Carruthers for some design input. An immediate friendship between John and Traveler Guitar blossomed and the end result is a completely updated line of beautiful and sophisticated instruments which exemplify Traveler Guitar's ingenuity and John Carruthers' attention to detail and extraordinary eye for beauty.

*From Left to right: MK-II Steel Natural,
EG1 Red Flame and Speedster Black*

Rick Turner's love for guitars began with his love for music in general – he was an amateur East Coast musician. After coming to terms with the future of his band – or lack thereof – he began building electric guitars. Six months after leaving the East Coast, Rolling Stone Magazine printed a rave review on his band.

Handmade is Not Easy Made

Turner's decision to hand-wind pickups was not due to respect for the hand-made instrument, or a desire to preserve age-old techniques – it was because he could not figure out where to buy them. This meant that he did not wind 8000+ turns like the machines could at Gibson or Fender, he had to stop around 1250 since his hands would cramp too badly to continue. The fortunate addition of Ron Wickersham to his team massively helped the tone of Turner guitars – Ron realized that these low-impedance pickups Rick was producing captured a much wider frequency band than the pickups on existing commercial instruments. Coupled with a pre-amp to boost the signal back to the levels achieved by high-impedance pickups, the result was an amplified guitar or bass with a much richer, more natural tone. Alembic Inc. was born.

Rick spent the next few years honing his craft and supplying instruments to various rock bands such as the Grateful Dead and the Stills. Alembic instruments have been spotted in the hands of Lamar Williams of The Allman Brothers Band, Tom Fowler of Frank Zappa and the Mothers of Invention, John Entwistle of The Who, and John Paul Jones of Led Zeppelin. He later left Alembic instruments to pursue his ambitions of designing his own Model One guitar, with a graphite neck design. This guitar would later be played by Fleetwood Mac's Lindsey Buckingham.

Rick has worked for Gibson's research and development department, among others, but after 1991 he returned to focus on building his own line of instruments. He had developed the Electroline Solidbody Bass for Gibson, but the idea was rejected and thus fell back into Rick's hands, so this was the fastest addition to his roster of models. The Electroline features Rick's Universal String Pickup, a piezo crystal pickup that responds both to the vertical pressure exerted by strings and to their horizontal vibrations. By coupling the responses of these two crystal configurations, he was able to get a much more three-dimensional signal from the original acoustic sound wave.

Left: Lindsey Buckingham of
Fleetwood Mac performs on his
Rick Turner guitar

Univox

Unicord Corporation bought the Amplifier Corporation of America of Westbury in the early 1960s and quickly began marketing a line of amplifiers under the name of Univox. This company was then purchased by Gulf + Western in 1967 and production was exported to Japan in 1975 where they continued to make guitars until 1982. A fire at the Matsumoku factory stopped production under the Univox name and production was moved yet again, to Korea, where the instruments were created under the make Westbury.

Various mergers took place during the life of Univox; in 1967 Unicord merged with Merson – an importer that made various headstock-brand guitars such as Tempo and Hagstrom. This new company was called Merson Muscle Products – A Division of Unicord Incoporated, a Gulf + Western Systems Company. A year later, they started producing Univox guitars but split in 1975. Unicord did continue to make guitars until their demise in 1978 and even added some newer models to the roster.

Musicians Resurrect Vintage Models

Univox did what many foreign production companies did, and borrowed designs from other companies such as Fender, Gibson and Epiphone. Collectors often refer to these models as 'lawsuit copies' due to the massive number of court cases that they caused when the design originators sued copy cats. The most famous of Univox's models is probably the Hi-Flier which was based on the Mosrite Ventures guitar – it gained notoriety through it's famous user, Kurt Cobain, almost two decades after original production stopped.

The Lucy

The Lucy – a vintage Univox – was originally produced in the 1960s and featured an unusual body of clear acrylic. It had 24 frets set in rosewood with dueling pickups and a maple neck. As Univox put it in an advertisement: "You'll love Lucy".

Valley Arts

Above: Larry Carlton & Steve Lukather, on their Valley Arts guitars

Valley Arts Guitar is an American electric guitar manufacturer currently owned and operated by Gibson. Mike McGuire and Al Carness founded the company in the mid-1970s in North Hollywood, California. The name "Valley Arts" is a reference to the firm's original location in the San Fernando Valley. Partners in a music store and repair shop, their repairs and customizations gained the attention of Los Angeles studio musicians and jazz guitarists such as Lee Ritenour, Steve Lukather, Tommy Tedesco and Larry Carlton. They finally began to build custom guitars from scratch in 1977, and within 6 years demand for these guitars was so high that they needed to open a separate manufacturing facility just to keep up. Most of their guitars had a radical styling similar to that of a Superstrat; others were modified versions of Fender's most popular designs, the Stratocaster and the Telecaster. "Signature" Valley Arts features often included highly-figured wood grain on the front, translucent colored finishes, gold hardware, Floyd Rose locking tremolos, EMG and Seymour Duncan humbucking pickups.

A fire destroyed their shop in 1990 and, since it was underinsured, McGuire and Carness sold it and chose to concentrate on the manufacturing side of the business. In an attempt at expansion, they sold half of their business to the Korean manufacturer Samick in 1992 but quickly lost interest with the venture due to dissatisfaction with their new positions in the company and the lower quality of products so they moved to Gibson in 1993. Gibson, although already a giant, was expanding and acquiring new businesses to diversify their brand, so in the late 1990s they also bought the Valley Arts brand to join their custom shop.

Over a decade after the fire, Valley Arts reopened as a music store, repair facility and small manufacturer specializing in custom guitars in downtown Nashville. Al Carness managed the store; Mike McGuire is operations manager of the Gibson Custom division, which oversees the Valley Arts line of guitars. The Nashville store closed in 2005.

Brent Mason Custom Signature

Produced through the Gibson Guitar Company, this Telecaster-like model is built of swamp ash with maple for its fingerboard and neck. Satin chrome locking Sperzel tuners add to the guitar's amenities as do the pickup variations which is a Gibson influenced exclusive: Gibson Mini-humbucker (neck position) Duncan Hot Stack (middle) and Duncan Vintage Lead Stack (bridge). The configuration allows for 3-way switching between the single coils and the one humbucker to give a tonal range that a traditional fender-style Telecaster would not and one that gives the Brent Mason a niche all its own.

Vox

Vox has a unique and particularly interesting heritage; the brand has been associated with top artists of the 1960s such as the Rolling Stones, the Beatles and the Shadows and was seen as one of the greatest innovators of music technology. It is one of the few to survive over 50 years of social, economic and musical change as well as 6 changes of ownership to thrive on the competitive market. Now there is a whole new generation of Vox users, many because of their aspirations and respect for the many artists who rely on Vox for their sound. Although Vox amps and other sound equipment is what brought them into the limelight, they have also maintained a large number of high quality electric guitars.

Virage by Vox

This is a series of semi-hollow bodied electrics produced by Vox. Vox went to town on the modern-day tools in guitar making to bring its visualization of a multi-versatile guitar to life utilizing three-dimensional cutting techniques to allow for maximum contour and ergonomic feel.

All models are equipped with a specially designed aluminum bridge. The Advanced Full Contact design allows the guitar player to deliver thick, rich tone with clear harmonics which allows near perfect intonation with any gauge string used. This is also a very light feature which is a great advance in lowering the overall bodyweight of the sometimes cumbersome electric guitar. As a semi-hollow, the Virage also sports some construction unique to acoustic guitars and sports an integral tonebar construction allowing for maximum sustain and resonance through the instrument.

A vast range of classic and modern tones is possible through Vox's 3-90 pickup system. This tech boasts the ability to mimic a P-90, humbucker, or single coil pickup without the use of active electronics or onboard battery of any kind. All analog technology is used. The Virage is also built with a differing style of neck joint; the long tenon joint. Similar to a set-in neck design, the long tenon creates greater contact area between materials and therefore, a stronger bond between parts.

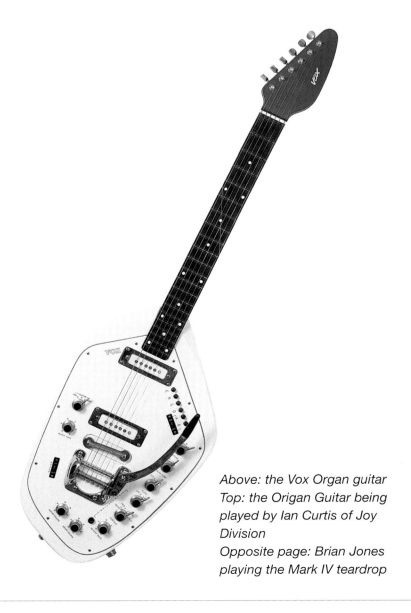

Above: the Vox Organ guitar
Top: the Origan Guitar being played by Ian Curtis of Joy Division
Opposite page: Brian Jones playing the Mark IV teardrop

Warwick

Hans-Peter Wilfer founded the Warwick Bass Guitar Company in Germany in 1982. They now offer more thatn 20 bass models and are renowned for their 'growling' tone and high quality tonewoods which are put together to create unorthodox models. Their use of rare woods even influenced their slogan 'The Sound of Wood'.

Warwick is one of the few companies to have maintained it's original home, and all instruments are still handcrafted in Germany, with the exception of the 'Alien' acoustic bass which is made in Korea. Since the 1990s, all electric basses use MEC pickups and electronics (SD Basslines are also available on certain models). Left-handed, "broadneck" and fretless versions are also available with four, five, six and seven strings.

Famous Faces Playing Basses

Both Jack Bruce and the late John Entwistle played and endorsed Warwick basses, and both have had custom-made signature models created for them by Warwick. Jack Bruce has the Jack Bruce Signature Thumb NT and the Jack Bruce CRB, while John Entwistle uses the LTD Buzzard. In 2005, Warwick introduced the Stryker; a replica of the Exploiter basses made for John by Alembic during John's Who days.

Many other celebrity players have had signature models made, such as Jonas Hellborg who recently had a semi acoustic bass created. The design is somewhat similar to his Wechter "Roman" bass, and he has taken to using these basses on tour as of 2006. Bassist P-Nut of 311 also has two signature models, which are based on his Streamer Stage II 5-strings called the P-Nut Signature and P-Nut II Signature.

Ex-Jamiroquai bassist Stuart Zender and Warwick have recently reunited to produce an exclusive Stuart Zender signature bass guitar. Zender is a longstanding fan of the Warwick brand and actually began his career by playing Warwick guitars in 1993, when Jamiroquai was formed. Zender endorsed Warwick during his Jamiroquai days, with Warwick designing and bringing him custom models such as the infamous Warwick Iroquai "rug" bass, the all white bass including blue LEDs, the Chrome "Ender" along with many other original Warwicks.

Opposite page: the Warwick Fortress bass guitar
Above: Prince performs on his Warwick guitar

Washburn

The Washburn guitar company started making guitars in 1883 in Chicago under the watchful eye of George Washburn Lyon. The factory would later be involved and located near a musical movement in Chicago in the 1920s. A new tone and voice was sweeping through America, sung by travelling musicians such as the Delta Blues who played in new venues every night. The foundations of rock 'n' roll would be laid, together with a new attitude towards the acoustic guitar. Washburn saw an opportunity with the blues, and moved to design guitars these players would want.

Washburn, while wanting to appeal to this very particular market, also benefited from geography. Maxwell Street, a hotbed of venues and blues clubs in the 1920s, sat only moments from where Washburn's first factory operated, so it was relatively easy to do market research – watching and listening to the musicians to find out what body styles and materials would best suit their needs. After they realized what their audience wanted, all that was left was to make it and let them play. As with many other brands, customers begot more customers as the specialty of these guitars was noticed. The history of Washburn Guitars is the history of a wide range of musicians. From blues players who shaped rock 'n' roll, to multi-platinum recording artists to emerging guitar virtuosos.

Washburn now makes almost every guitar imaginable: electric guitars, acoustic guitars, electric basses, acoustic basses, banjos, mandolins, travel guitars, and amplifiers. The company also makes accessories including guitar cases, clothing, and other parts like tuners, pickups, and straps. Despite this wide variety, Washburn is not a jack of all trades (and a master of none) and is mostly known for its electric guitars and acoustic guitars. The Vintage series is a retelling of that exciting time in the history of Washburn when the guitar and musical world were in flux, brimming with new ideas and innovation. Newly formed companies are at a disadvantage with this particular design only having the ability to craft "vintage style" instruments of bygone eras that they did not participate in but Washburn was there, at the forefront, and is able to use the participation as a selling point.

The Paul Stanley Signature

Paul Stanley from Kiss collaborated with Washburn to create a signature series of electric and acoustic guitars designed by Paul himself. The Washburn PS7000 electric guitar features a mahogany set neck and mahogany body, a rosewood fingerboard with trapezoid inlays, 2 Egnater humbucker pickups, a tune-o-matic bridge and stop tailpiece. With an eye-catching body shape and amazing gloss finish, this guitar sets itself apart in very much the same way the arena rockers have for decades.

*Opposite page and far right:
the N4 Vintage
Below, PS1800B*

Weissenborn

Hermann Weissenborn manufacturered the Weissenborn lap slide guitar in Los Angeles in the 1920s and 1930s. These guitars are now highly collectable and created a template around which most non-resonator acoustic lap steel guitars are currently produced. It is estimated that fewer than 5000 original instruments were created and it is unknown how many now survive. Both single and twin neck models were produced, both with highly adapted bodies that run the full length of the fingerboards, making conventional upright playing completely impossible. The brand is now used for reproduction instruments, based largely upon the instruments that brought them into the limelight.

Tone Is Always the Issue

Hawaiian guitar players still hanker after their own Weissenborn guitar and almost 80 years after the last one was made, the Weissenborn has enjoyed a curious amount of staying power thanks to modern day musicians keeping it alive around the world.

Ben Harper is a perfect example of just such a musician; playing Weissenborns since he first broke into music as a solo artist, and is now one of the best known endorsers of the brand. He performs with a huge collection of slide guitars and Weissenborns, which he exploits fantastically due to this expertise and knowledge of the instruments' tonal qualities. The Weissenborn steel is also inspiring and plays a major role in the careers of new musical talent, such as Xavier Rudd, John Butler or Andrew Winton.

Since being brought to public attention in the 1990s, luthiers and guitar builders are making new Weissenborn based instruments, both acoustics and electric lap steel models; Asher Guitars, David Dart, Emmanuel Romont, Christophe Grellier and many others make custom orders and special slide-guitar series, basing their designs on the beautiful Weissenborn shape. It has helped, by extension, the revival of the full lap slide style guitars, including Dobro - helped of course by the fact that Hendrix performed Voodoo Child on a lapsteel.

Opposite page: Ben Harper, on his
Weissenborn lap steel guitar

Xotic

Based in Los Angeles, Xotic's mother company, PCI, exports high quality American-made guitars, pickups, amps, effects and accessories, but Xotic began their journey by creating customized basses. Their subsidiary, PCI Japan, also markets these products all over Japan.

Xotic History

Xotic began in 1996 as a manufacturer of high quality customized basses. Xotic Basses have been well received by professional bassists such as Michael Rhodes, Keith Horn, Ric Fierabracci and Chris Roy.

In 1999, they introduced a new line of guitar/bass pedals, Xotic Effects. The now infamous RC and AC Boosters have the privilege of being on some of the most famous pedal boards today. Thanks to their superior sound and transparency, the many live acts have come to depend on Xotic pedals for their signature sound.

Xotic's place in the electric guitar world is a similar one held by Vox or Line 6. With the amplifier and the pickup comes distortion and with all sound being under music's province it is then sought out to be manipulated by the musician. A guitar player's search for the perfect tone is unending and many accumulate vast stacks of "effects pedals" boxes that alter the sound pushed through the speakers and out into the world, throughout their musical careers. Effects boards like the ones created by Xotic push all of these pedals into one digital processor thereby eliminating all the gear a guitar player has to lug around from gig to gig.

Opposite page: professional Bassist Michael Rhodes

Yamaha has been an innovator and designer of everything from keyboards, to guitars, to motorcycles. There is seemingly nothing on the map that they cannot grasp hold of and bend to their will. As a company they have been building musical instruments since the late 1800s. In 1942, they debuted their first acoustic guitar. By then, the company had been in business for almost 50 years, so they were already known for their instruments and musical products. Yamahas product line has since expanded. At one point, they even had an archery products business.

The E Series

The E Series is an original Yamaha design from the '60s. The guitar has 3 single coil pickups, vintage vibrato system, 5 position switch, tremolo bar. The neck is made from maple with a samurai headstock and a rosewood fingerboard, complimented by a basswood body.

The RGX Series

This body design by Yamaha features hard-edge design and ultimate playability. The new RGX520FZ and RGX320FZ are Yamaha's first true double-cutaway set neck guitars with features and appointments typically found only on custom guitars. The instrument features an elegant carved top with body binding, a mahogany neck with a bound rosewood fingerboard, 3-D headstock design, two Yamaha humbucking pickups, and chrome hardware with Yamaha's signature tailpieces.

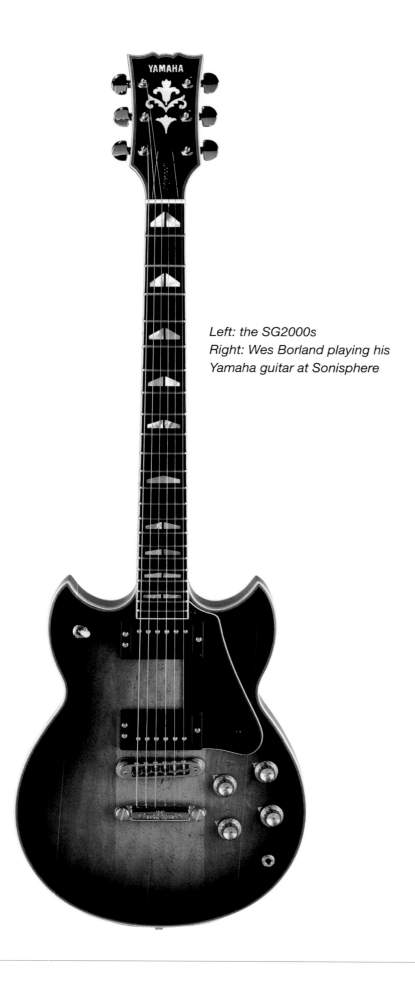

Left: the SG2000s
Right: Wes Borland playing his Yamaha guitar at Sonisphere

English-born Tony Zemaitis constantly designed and built as a child – everything fascinated him, from model airplanes to handmade bicycles. His creative talents first led him to cabinetry where he learned invaluable skills in working with wood, design and decoration.

In the 1950s, as a young guitar player, Tony was unsatisfied with the available guitars of the times. So taking cues from a friend's classical guitar, he decided to build his own - the first ever Zemaitis guitar. From then on, he has honed his craft and meticulously designed beautiful guitars by experimenting with new designs and materials to constantly improve the standard of his work. He attracted the initial interest of the London blues and folk scene where he played his instruments and hung out with other musicians of that sphere. Slowly those around him began to ask questions and inquire who made his guitars.

By the 1980s, his reputation for workmanship, styling, playability and tonal quality had made Tony Zemaitis a living legend. While highly coveted by collectors, Tony didn't restrict his customers to just the rich and famous and always remained true to his ideals. Though he worked primarily by himself, producing just a handful of guitars every year, Tony was just as happy to work with enthusiastic amateur guitarists and even sold "student" grade models to those with lower budgets.

It was the combination of quality, craftsmanship, innovation and simply beautiful instruments that have expanded Tony's fan base to span across the world. After 40 years of handcrafting fine guitars and having virtually created the "boutique guitar," Tony retired in 2000 and passed away shortly after in 2002.

The Pearl Front

A trademark of the Zemaitis design, pearl front electric guitars are inlaid in mother of pearl on the guitar's top which sits over Honduran mahogany. The fingerboard is ebony, resting just above the guitar's single cutaway body. DiMarzio humbucking pickups outfit the guitar with enough firepower to sustain low-level barrages of growl which belies the shifting boundary of color that the pearl's top gives off.

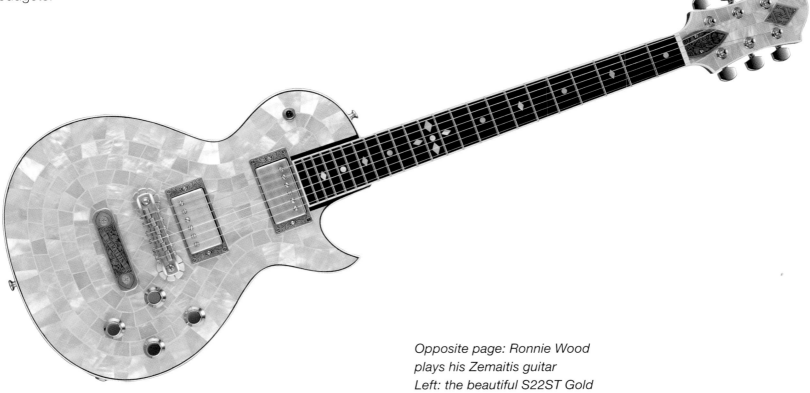

Opposite page: Ronnie Wood plays his Zemaitis guitar
Left: the beautiful S22ST Gold

Guitar Timeline

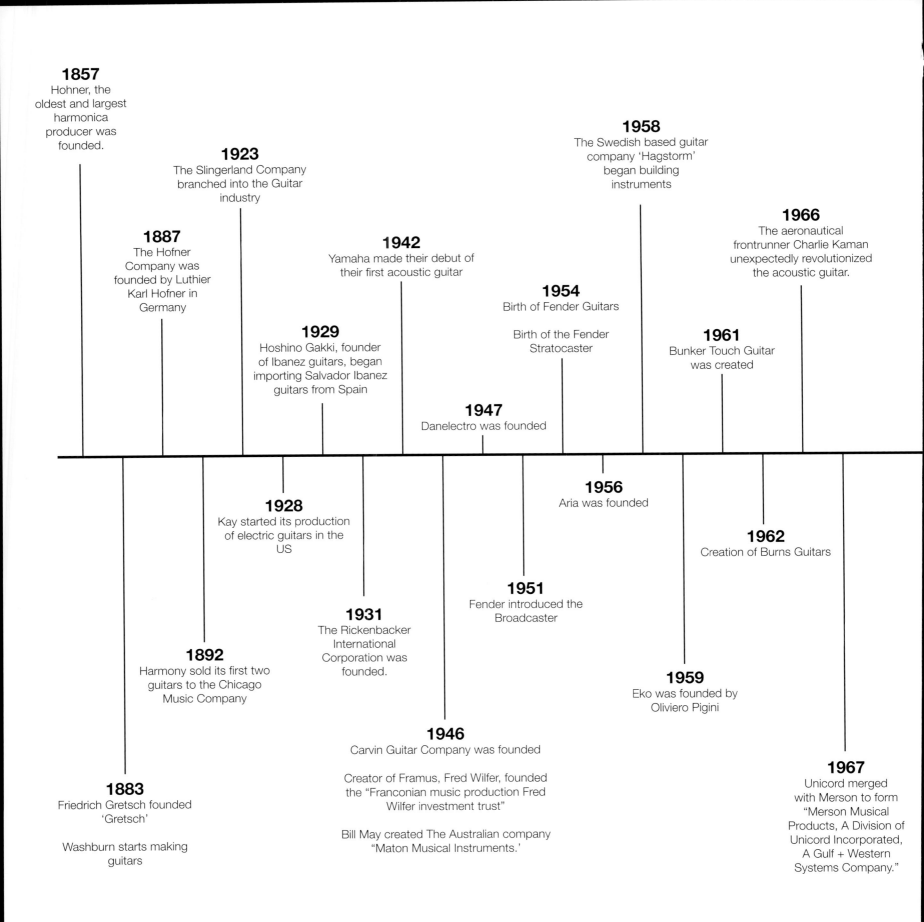

1857
Hohner, the oldest and largest harmonica producer was founded.

1923
The Slingerland Company branched into the Guitar industry

1887
The Hofner Company was founded by Luthier Karl Hofner in Germany

1942
Yamaha made their debut of their first acoustic guitar

1958
The Swedish based guitar company 'Hagstorm' began building instruments

1966
The aeronautical frontrunner Charlie Kaman unexpectedly revolutionized the acoustic guitar.

1954
Birth of Fender Guitars

Birth of the Fender Stratocaster

1929
Hoshino Gakki, founder of Ibanez guitars, began importing Salvador Ibanez guitars from Spain

1961
Bunker Touch Guitar was created

1947
Danelectro was founded

1928
Kay started its production of electric guitars in the US

1956
Aria was founded

1962
Creation of Burns Guitars

1931
The Rickenbacker International Corporation was founded.

1951
Fender introduced the Broadcaster

1892
Harmony sold its first two guitars to the Chicago Music Company

1959
Eko was founded by Oliviero Pigini

1946
Carvin Guitar Company was founded

Creator of Framus, Fred Wilfer, founded the "Franconian music production Fred Wilfer investment trust"

Bill May created The Australian company "Maton Musical Instruments.'

1883
Friedrich Gretsch founded 'Gretsch'

Washburn starts making guitars

1967
Unicord merged with Merson to form "Merson Musical Products, A Division of Unicord Incorporated, A Gulf + Western Systems Company."

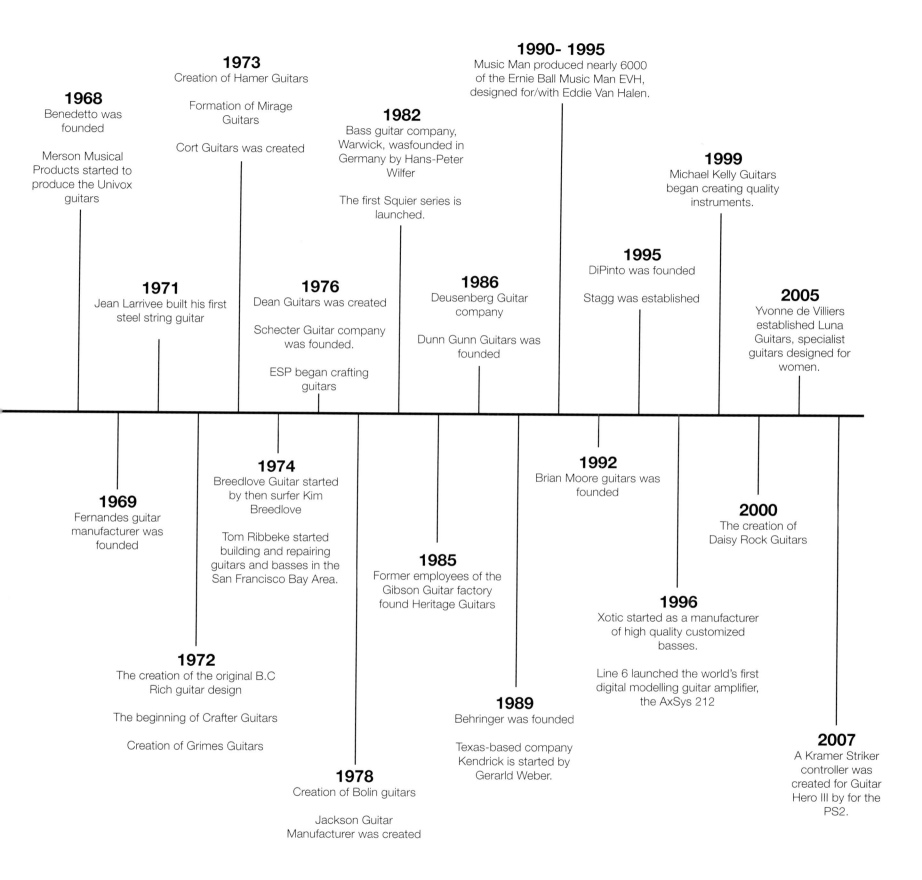

1968
Benedetto was founded

Merson Musical Products started to produce the Univox guitars

1973
Creation of Hamer Guitars

Formation of Mirage Guitars

Cort Guitars was created

1982
Bass guitar company, Warwick, wasfounded in Germany by Hans-Peter Wilfer

The first Squier series is launched.

1990- 1995
Music Man produced nearly 6000 of the Ernie Ball Music Man EVH, designed for/with Eddie Van Halen.

1999
Michael Kelly Guitars began creating quality instruments.

1971
Jean Larrivee built his first steel string guitar

1976
Dean Guitars was created

Schecter Guitar company was founded.

ESP began crafting guitars

1986
Deusenberg Guitar company

Dunn Gunn Guitars was founded

1995
DiPinto was founded

Stagg was established

2005
Yvonne de Villiers established Luna Guitars, specialist guitars designed for women.

1969
Fernandes guitar manufacturer was founded

1974
Breedlove Guitar started by then surfer Kim Breedlove

Tom Ribbeke started building and repairing guitars and basses in the San Francisco Bay Area.

1985
Former employees of the Gibson Guitar factory found Heritage Guitars

1992
Brian Moore guitars was founded

2000
The creation of Daisy Rock Guitars

1972
The creation of the original B.C Rich guitar design

The beginning of Crafter Guitars

Creation of Grimes Guitars

1989
Behringer was founded

Texas-based company Kendrick is started by Gerarld Weber.

1996
Xotic started as a manufacturer of high quality customized basses.

Line 6 launched the world's first digital modelling guitar amplifier, the AxSys 212

1978
Creation of Bolin guitars

Jackson Guitar Manufacturer was created

2007
A Kramer Striker controller was created for Guitar Hero III by for the PS2.

Acknowledgements

Getty Picture Library

9, 14, 15, 18, 19, 24, 25, 30, 31, 37, 42, 43, 44, 45, 48, 49,
58, 62, 63, 64, 67, 69, 74, 75, 76, 77, 78, 88, 89, 90, 91, 92,
93, 94, 100, 101, 112, 113, 105, 121, 125, 141, 146, 147,
14, 150, 151, 156, 157, 158, 159, 160, 162, 163, 171, 173,
183, 184, 192, 196, 197, 198, 201, 204, 207, 208, 209, 210.

Istock Picture Library

16, 21, 22, 29, 34, 38, 51, 55, 56, 71, 81, 99, 104, 106, 109,
118, 126, 131, 133, 138, 142, 145, 164, 166, 175, 178, 179,
181, 188, 191, 194, 195, 206.

Balafon Image Bank, Managed by Jawbone Press

71, 72, 85, 120, 133, 172, 180.

Garth Blore

14, 29, 46, 47, 54, 79, 162, 186, 199.

XOX 6, 7

Aria 10, 11

Austin 12, 13

Bunker 26

Charvel 32, 33

Daisy Rock 40, 41

Dean 44

Eastwood 52, 53

Epiphone 58, 59, 60, 61

Fender 65, 66

Gretsch 82, 83

Grimshaw 86, 87

Highland 96, 97

Hohner 102, 103

Jackson 107

Johnson 110, 111

Kay 116, 117

Kona 122, 123

Larrive 128, 129

Luna 134, 135

Manson 136, 137

Mirage 143

Novax 152

Organic 154, 155

Robin 168, 169

Squier 176, 177

Takamine 185

Traveler 191

Warwick 200

Washburn 202, 203

Zemaitis 211

Glossary

A

Abalone – an ornate shell material commonly used on instrument inlays. Abalone inlays come in a rainbow of colors and can appear to change color when viewed from different angles. Sometimes also called "mother of pearl".

Action - the string height above the tops of the frets.

Active - when pickups are said to be active they incorporate a pre-amp which requires additional power. The result is a boost and/or wider range for the pickup.

Archtop - a guitar which has been carved or pressed. The bridge and tailpiece are movable. Generally used by Jazz musicians.

Bakelite - early form of plastic used in some guitars from the 30s to the 50s.

Bigsby - a simple non-recessed vibrato developed by Paul Bigsby.

B

Binding - a protective and decorative strip made of wood or plastic that is placed along the outer most edges of the top, back, neck, fingerboard and some times headstock. This is a cap used to seal and protect joints. Sometimes incorrectly referred to as purfling, purfling actually refers to inlays along side of the binding and not the actual binding itself.

Block Markers - square, rectangular or shark tooth inlays marking fingerboard position.

Body - the main portion of the guitar which the controls, bridge and pickups are mounted.

Bolt On - an instrument that has its neck attached by bolts rather than being glued in place.

Bookmatched - most acoustic and many archtop guitars have tops and backs that are 2 pieces of wood glued together to form one large panel. Bookmatched refers to the wood coming from the same tree and actually being one piece of wood that has been but into consecutive slices so the grain in the panels creates mirror image patterns.

Brace - wooden struts glued to the insides of hollowbody guitars providing strength and affecting tone quality. An X-brace is a popular brace pattern used in hollowbody guitars. Other bracing patterns include the ladder brace, fan bracing and scalloped braces.

Bridge - bridges come in a variety of shapes and sizes. On a solid body electric guitar they generally fixed and hold the saddle that makes contact with the strings. On archtop guitars the bridge is usually held in place only by the tension of the strings and can be easily moved, also called a "floating bridge".

Bridge Pins – pins that anchor the strings on to the bridge

C

CAP - a common electrical component that stores up an electrical charge generally used on the tone potentiometer on electric guitars.

Celluloid - plastic material used on guitar pickguards, tuners and binding. This material is not very durable and deteriorates over time therefore many vintage guitars have issues with celluloid parts.

Center Block - the solid wood block running through the body of a semi-acoustic guitar body.

Checking - cracking found in lacquer finished guitars. Vintage guitars often have checking in their lacquer finishes caused by the guitar's wood expanding and contracting with changes in temperature and humidity.

Cutaway – a guitar which has been cut away to allow easy access to the frets while reaching over the body. A double cut guitar away has both sides cut away. Usually referred to as "singlecut" and "doublecut" guitars.

D

Dog Ear - a P-90 style pickup with mounting ears.

Dot Neck – a guitar with simple dot inlays in the neck position markers.

Glossary

E

Electro Acoustic - an acoustic guitar with a built in pickup, often a piezo electric pickup.

End block - acoustic guitars normally have an end block and a neck block at opposite ends of the body. The end block is usually glued to the top, back, and sides at the bottom end of the guitar. Often strap buttons are are anchored into this block as it provides the strength necessary to support a strap.

F

F-hole - an "f" shaped sound hole on some hollowbody and semi-acoustic guitars.

Fingerboard (also called a fretboard) - the surface of the neck that contains the frets. Note there are also some guitars that are "fretless" but the fingerboard is still used without frets. The fingerboard is generally a separate piece of wood glued to the neck. It's often made of a hard durable wood as the frets must be securely anchored into the fretboard. Vintage guitars often used Brazilian Rosewood and Ebony for fingerboard material.

Finish - the protective coating covering the guitar, often paint or lacquer.

Fixed Bridge - non-vibrato bridges.

Flame - sometimes also called Flame Top. Generally refers to Maple with dramatic grain resembling flames.

Flat Top - an acoustic guitar with a flat (non-arched) top. Many Martin and Gibson guitars are considered flat top acoustic guitars.

Fret - metal wire inlayed at intervals along the fingerboard. The guitar player presses down on the string forcing the string to touch the fret changing the sting length and producing different notes. There are a variety of fret wire profiles used for frets.

H

Hang Tag - small tags and cards hung on guitars in show rooms. A hang tag for a vintage guitar is generally very difficult to find.

Hard Tail - an electric guitar without a vibrato bridge, often used to describe Fender guitars.

Headstock - the part of the guitar where the strings attach to the tuners.

Heel - portion of neck where the neck curves or is reduced to join the body.

Hollow Body - an electric guitar body style with a thin body similar to an acoustic guitar.

Humbucker - a noise canceling twin coil pickup.

I

Inlay – the decorative material that is cut and embedded into the body, neck or headstock of a guitar.

Intonation - the guitars ability to play in tune at various positions along the neck. Often adjusted by adjusting the bridge saddle.

J

Jackplate - mounting plate for output jack.

L

Laminated - the backs, sides and even tops of some instruments can be made from several pieces of wood which have been laminated to form one piece, usually at the expense of sound quality.

Locking Nut - bolts that lock the strings in place at the nut.

Luthier - a guitar maker and guitar repair expert.

M

Machine Heads - also knows as tuners or tuning machines. Allows string tension to be changed changing the pitch of the strings.

N

Neck Block - the neck block is found inside of the body at the base of the neck. The Neck block provides a strong point to mount the neck to the body.

Neck Plate - a metal plate used in the Fender style bolt on designs, it is screwed to the neck and the body fastening the neck to the guitar body.

Neck Pickup - the pickup closest to the neck.

Neck Reset - a neck reset is performed restore the correct angle between the fingerboard bridge which provides the correct action needed to play the guitar.

Neck Press - gentle heat and pressure used to straighten a neck.

Nut - located at the end of the fingerboard before the headstock, used to provide proper string height and spacing before the strings enter the tuners.

P

P-90 - an early Gibson single coil pickup.

PAF - a sticker on Gibson pickups.

Passive - a guitar that does not use pickups which require power (active pickups).

Peghead - where the tuners are mounted, also called a headstock.

Pickguard - also called a scratchplate, a thin covering screwed or glued to the top of a guitar to protect the guitar from picks and fingernails. Comes in a variety of colors and styles. Often cracked around the screw holes on vintage guitars.

Pot - a Potentiometer mounted to the body of an electric guitar commonly used for control of volume and tone. The tone pot will normally have a CAP soldered in circuit.

Pre-CBS - Fender guitars manufactured before the 1965 takeover of Fender by CBS. Vintage collectors prefer pre-CBS guitars.

Q

Quilted - beautiful undulating patterns found in wood, generally refers to Maple and can also be referred to as "maple quilting" or maple quilted".

R

Relief - upward arching bow in an instrument's neck that allows the strings to move without touching the frets. A bowed or warped neck will have to be heated and pressed to restore the neck to correct relief.

Refin - a refinished guitar. Refinished guitars have a significantly lower value than original guitar with the original surface.

Refret - also called a fret job, refers to re-fretting a guitar.

Rout - a hole or cavity cut into a guitar, often the body of the guitar. Many times a pickup cavity is routed to enable a different pickup to be installed. Routing will diminish the value of a vintage guitar and routing should not be done on a valuable guitar.

Rosette - The decorative strip or inlay work found around the soundhole on an acoustic guitar.

S

Saddle - the part of the bridge where the strings make contact transferring the string vibration to the bridge and body of the guitar.

Scale Length - length of the vibrating string from nut to saddle or twice the distance from the nut to the 12th fret.

Glossary

Set Neck - a neck that is glued into the body and uses no bolts for attachment.

Single Coil Pickup - an early pickup design with a single coil of wire wrapped around a magnet.

Solid Body - refers to electric guitars with a solid (non-hollow) body.

Sound Hole - hole in the top of the body of a hollow body guitar. May enhance sound of be simply for looks. An F-Hole is a type of sound hole.

Sustain - Length of time a string vibrates

Split Coil - a double coil pickup wound with multiple coils that are smaller than a standard 2 coil pickup where each coil works with a few strings.

Stop Tailpiece - also called a stud tailpiece. Fixed to the top of the guitar and anchors the strings to the top. Holes in the tailpiece allow strings to pass thru the stop tailpiece and over the bridge.

T

T- Frets - the shape of the metal fret. T-Frets are used in most refrets.

Tailpiece - on instruments without bridge pins the strings are commonly anchored to a tailpiece. This normally mounts to the end block and pulls the strings down towards the top after passing across the bridge.

Thinline - hollow body electric guitars, first used with the Gibson Byrdland guitar.

Through Neck - a Thru neck design uses a neck that actually runs right thru the middle of the body.

Trapeze Tailpiece - tailpiece design that has a hinge like mechanism on it and has a shape similar to a swinging trapeze.

Tremolo - another term used for Vibrato or Tremolo Arm

Truss Rod - a rod that runs through the middle of a guitar's

neck below the fingerboard. The truss rod helps to stiffen the neck and prevent bowing caused by the tension caused by the strings.

Truss Rod Cover - a decorative cover that covers up the access point for adjusting the truss rod.

Thumbwheel - a small wheel used on adjustable bridges (those usually found on archtop guitars or mandolins) to adjust the bridges height. The top portion of an adjustable bridge rest upon these flat wheels and as they are screwed upward on their post the top portion of the bridge is raised.

Tune-o-matic - this bridge is commonly found on Les Paul style electric guitars. It sits on two thumbwheels and has six saddles which allow individual intonation adjustment for each string.

Tuning Machines - mechanical devices used to increase or decrease string tension.

V

Veneer - thin wood or plastic laminate used in the construction of some guitars.

Vibrato – the bridge and/or tailpiece which can alter the pitch of strings when the vibrato arm is pressed. Also called a whammy bar.

Volute - a piece of wood installed just behind the peghead. It strengthens the neck where the headstock begins.

*Hutchins 6-neck guitar aptly
named "The Beast"*

Index